P9-DHS-340

12⁵⁰

Confronting the Horror

CONFRONTING THE HORROR

The Novels of Nelson Algren

James R. Giles

THE KENT STATE UNIVERSITY PRESS

Kent, Ohio, and London, England

© 1989 by The Kent State University Press, Kent, Ohio 44242
All rights reserved
Library of Congress Catalog Card Number 83–311000
ISBN 0–87338–378–8
Manufactured in the United States of America

Library of Congress Cataloging-in-Publication Data

Giles, James Richard, 1937–
  Confronting the horror : the novels of Nelson Algren / James R. Giles.
      p.   cm.
  Bibliography: p.
  Includes index.
  ISBN 0–87338–378–8 (alk. paper) ∞
  1. Algren, Nelson, 1909–   —Criticism and interpretation.
2. Naturalism in literature.   I. Title.
PS3501.L4625Z68   1989
813'.52—dc19   89–31100
                                                                                    CIP

British Library Cataloging-in-Publication data are available.

Contents

Preface and
Acknowledgments

Several influential critics have in recent years written obituaries for the tradition of American literary naturalism. Extensive reading in post–World War II American fiction reveals, however, that this tradition still retains vitality, although literary and philosophical movements which developed later in the twentieth century have inevitably influenced and modified it. That American literary naturalism has proven to be receptive to innovation and change should not be surprising. Such major scholars of the tradition as Charles Child Walcutt and Donald Pizer have demonstrated convincingly that naturalism *as practiced* was never as scientific and clinical as the theoretical essays of Emile Zola, Frank Norris, and others proclaimed. Walcutt, in *American Literary Naturalism: A Divided Stream* (1956) points to the romantic, and at times mystical, overtones of the fiction of Norris, Jack London, Stephen Crane, Theodore Dreiser, and the turn-of-the-century American naturalists.

A contemporary naturalism, which focuses on urban slum-dwelling and other social outcasts and which emphasizes environmental determinism while incorporating crucial aspects and techniques of literary modernism, Sartrian existentialism, and Céline's vision of the 'absurd,' has emerged in post–World War II American fiction. It has, after all, been virtually impossible for any post–World War II writer to ignore the influences of James Joyce, T. S. Eliot, Virginia Woolf, Jean-Paul Sartre, Albert Camus, and

Céline. Yet, perhaps because naturalism seems *in theory* antithetical to modernism and literary existentialism, little critical attention has been paid to the emergence of a post–World War II American naturalism. In fact, the term *naturalist* in much modern literary criticism virtually functions as a synonym for *old-fashioned* and *outdated*. While it is not difficult to explain, this phenomenon is shortsighted and has contributed to the critical neglect of several American writers who first achieved prominence in the late 1940s and early 1950s through novels utilizing techniques associated with naturalism. "The Unfound Generation," a term coined by James Jones in his novel *Some Came Running,* might be applied to these writers; the career of Nelson Algren best exemplifies the neglect which they have received. It is perhaps no coincidence that Algren's fiction, as much as that of any other American writer, was central to the emergence of a contemporary naturalism. (June Howard uses the term *latter-day naturalism* to describe the fiction of Hubert Selby, Jr.)

To be sure, Algren has always been an enigmatic figure. Even at the peak of his career, critics generally did not know what to make of him. In *Advertisements for Myself,* Norman Mailer describes him as "the Grand Odd-Ball" of American writers. In ways that will be examined later, Algren himself was partially responsible for such confusion. Generally, though, he was the victim of a continuing critical misperception. From the first, Algren was viewed as a disciple of Dreiser devoted to the documentation of external reality and to social protest. Especially in his early work, he was in fact influenced by Dreiser and by the Russian novelist, Alexandre Kuprin. A quotation from *Yama,* Kuprin's exposé of prostitution in czarist Russia, introduces part 1 of Algren's 1949 novel, *The Man With The Golden Arm:* "Do you understand, gentlemen, that all the horror is in just this—that there is no horror!"

For Algren, as for Kuprin, there was a strictly socioeconomic dimension to "the horror." He never wavered in his commitment to the lumpenproletariat, society's despised outcasts. Still, over the years Algren's vision of the horror evolved significantly. He was Jean-Paul Sartre's friend and Simone de Beauvoir's lover; and, prior to his involvement with the Sartre circle, he discovered the fiction of Céline. In Algren's best work, the horror reflects despair over the absurd nature of man and the obscenity of death at least as much as it expresses outrage at social and economic injustice. There are, then, two primary dimensions to the horror for Algren—external oppression and internal anxiety and dread. The critics who have dismissed him as an outdated naturalist are so preoccupied by the external horror in a novel such as *The Man With the Golden Arm* that they overlook Algren's exploration of the internal dread. It should be emphasized now that Sartre and de Beauvoir were not blind to this aspect of Algren's aesthetic.

In this study, I wish to examine two interrelated ideas—that Algren's novels are thematically richer and more complex than they are generally regarded as being and that they represent the work of an important American writer. After looking more closely at the postwar crisis of naturalism and at Algren's aesthetic indebtedness to Kuprin, Sartre, and Céline, I will discuss Algren's five novels and his 1963 miscellany, *Who Lost an American?*, in order to clarify his evolving concept of the horror.

In a concluding chapter, I will discuss Algren's novels in relation to what came before and what has appeared since. That is, I will discuss his fiction in relation to Maxim Gorky's seminal exploration of "the lower depths" and then look briefly at two contemporary writers, Hubert Selby, Jr., and John Rechy, who combine naturalistic technique with a largely existential, absurdist vision. Like Algren, Selby and Rechy generally depict a distinctly lower-class urban despair. Sharing a profound realization of the city's power to dehumanize the social and economic outcast, they emphasize, nevertheless, a horror, the source of which is as much internal as external. I will conclude with some suggestions about Algren's place in the emergence of a contemporary or latter-day naturalism and thus in a revised, more class-conscious, American literary canon. In this concluding chapter, I will not be concerned with the question of influence. Instead, I want to emphasize that the novels of Nelson Algren represent a crucial stage in the evolution of a vital body of contemporary American fiction.

I wish to thank several people for their contributions to this book. Martha Heasley Cox gave me excellent advice on the manuscript and generous encouragement on the project. Frederick C. Stern's exceptionally thorough reading of the manuscript resulted in a number of improvements. Babette Inglehart's invitation to participate in "Writing in the First Person: Nelson Algren 1909–1981," a symposium sponsored by the Chicago Public Library and the *Chicago Tribune,* allowed me to exchange ideas about Algren with Michael Anania, Martha Cox, Bettina Drew, and Roger Groening. I am also grateful for the special concern for my book shown by Jeanne West of the Kent State University Press. Cheryl Fuller and Karen Blaser valiantly typed the manuscript from my handwriting, and Florence Cunningham's editing of the final manuscript was detailed and intelligent. Finally, this book would simply not have been possible without the advice and support of Wanda H. Giles to whom it is dedicated.

Evolution of
"The Horror"

*T*hree months before Nelson Algren died in May of 1981, he had been elected to the American Institute of Arts and Letters. Yet he had failed to find an American publisher willing to offer an acceptable advance for his last novel, *The Devil's Stocking.* This paradoxical ending was in keeping with much of Algren's career. Because of his grim descriptions of Chicago's Polish-American slums in *Never Come Morning* and *The Man With the Golden Arm,* he was commonly viewed as a Chicago novelist in the tradition of Dreiser and Richard Wright. Yet, he was born in Detroit and died on Long Island. Moreover, the principal action of three of his five novels occurs outside Chicago, and he wrote convincingly about New Orleans and southwest Texas.

Algren's final significance as a writer is of more concern than his regional identification; and, despite his election to the Academy of Arts and Letters, there is no critical consensus about his importance. Algren won the first National Book Award for his 1949 novel, *The Man With the Golden Arm,* and was acclaimed by none other than Ernest Hemingway as ranking behind only William Faulkner among American novelists. After his 1956 novel, *A Walk on the Wild Side,* he was castigated by Leslie Fiedler and Norman Podhoretz, among other representatives of the critical establishment, as a sentimental, if not irresponsible, practitioner of naturalistic excess. *Walk* was the last Algren novel published during his lifetime, and he is ignored in such seminal studies of post–World War II American fiction as Tony Tanner's *City of Words* (1971), Josephine Hendin's *Vulnerable People* (1978), and John W. Aldridge's *The American Novel and the Way We Live Now* (1983). Ironically, Ihab Hassan's path-breaking *Radical Innocence* (1961), which initially proclaimed existentialism as the dominant influence on post–World War II American fiction, also ignores Algren. Hassan, Tanner, Hendin, and Aldridge have been influential in establishing the accepted canon of contemporary American writers.

Besides Hemingway, Algren has had other sympathetic and perceptive critics, among them George Bluestone, Maxwell Geismar, Malcolm Cowley, Lawrence Lipton, and Ralph J. Gleason. Still, the author of *Never Come Morning* and *The Man With the Golden Arm* has been poorly served by scholars and critics. This disservice arises from a fundamental misperception of the nature and content of Algren's fiction.

Fiedler and Podhoretz were neither the first nor the last critics to label Algren a naturalist and to assume that American literary naturalism is a static tradition incapable of evolving beyond its origins in the fiction of Theodore Dreiser, Frank Norris, and Stephen Crane. Such an assumption implies naturalism's acceptance of specific literary techniques and socioliterary goals. Fundamentally, American literary naturalism is thought to rest upon a belief in environmental determinism and a commitment to a scientific documentation of external reality. That these central tenets can exist along with an intensely romantic allegiance to the lower classes is obvious to any reader of the fiction of Jack London. Thus, social protest is often implicit in traditional literary naturalism.

Since World War II, the nature of reality has seemed increasingly nebulous. In fact, the very existence of a traditional reality is now debated by novelists and critics alike. If reality cannot be verified with certainty, it obviously is outside the realm of scientific documentation. The prime threat to man is then transformed into something simultaneously less tangible and more cosmically threatening than environment. Consequently, social protest is increasingly viewed as a hopeless, even ludicrous, act. Naturalism in the Dreiser-Norris sense becomes an outmoded tradition and anyone (supposedly anyone like Algren) who persists in following it a quaint anachronism. Not only naturalism, but realism itself is passé. According to John Barth, we need instead "novels which imitate the form of the Novel, by an author who imitates the role of Author" (275).

Tanner's critical study, *City of Words,* had an important and immediate effect upon the accepted canon of post–World War II American fiction. The controlling assumptions of Tanner's study inevitably lead him to conclude that metafiction as practiced by Barth and others constitutes the most valid route for the contemporary novelist to take. A reorientation to landscape has been required of the contemporary writer, Tanner argues. The questioning of external reality has forced the postwar novelist to turn inward and confront a landscape of chaotic consciousness and the subconscious.

Tanner argues that Russian-born émigré Vladimir Nabokov and Argentinian writer Jorge Luis Borges have exerted the most dramatic influence on contemporary American writers. Nabokov's fiction is characterized by elaborate linguistic exercises and experiments with the device of works within works. In part, these self-consciously intellectual experiments constitute a retreat from a focus upon external socioeconomic reality. As illustrated by the title of Borges's best-known collection, *Labyrinths,* his landscape is, if anything, more elaborately cerebral than Nabokov's. One of Borges's best-known stories, "The Library of Babel," begins "The universe (which others call the Library) . . . " (51) and contains this passage: "The certitude that everything has been written negates us or turns us into phantoms. . . . I suspect that the human species—the unique species—is about to be extinguished, but the Library will endure: illuminated, solitary, infinite, perfectly motionless, equipped with precious volumes, useless, incorruptible, secret" (58). *Infinite, useless,* and *secret* are perhaps the key terms from this description of Borges's allegory of the universe. Like his American disciples, Barth, Vonnegut, and Pynchon, Borges believes that our age of limitless technology generates infinite information (much of it contradictory), but little true knowledge or wisdom. The terms *useless* and *secret* imply that even the slightest comprehension of the universe of the library is a private, individual matter of no applicability to external reality. Labyrinths and mirrors are the pervasive metaphors for Borges's landscape of dreams and nightmares. Other Borges tales, such as "Tlön, Uqbor, Orbis Tertius," are essentially elaborate explorations of arcane "facts" about imaginary planets and worlds.

The library and the encyclopedia become for Borges the essential but perennially disappointing guides to meaningful truth and understanding. His declaration that "the certitude that everything has been written . . . turns us into phantoms" is, of course, quite close to the central assumptions behind John Barth's literature of exhaustion. The American exponents of metafiction also believe that external reality has been so thoroughly explored that there is nothing left to discover out there. It is, then, time to turn inward and explore dreams and nightmares or imaginary worlds like Vonnegut's Tralfamadore; and the realistic-naturalistic tradition is inadequate for such exploration.

Especially as an argument for dismissing Algren, however, this widely shared analysis of the death of the realistic-naturalistic tradition has at least three basic fallacies. As mentioned, both in its genesis in the turn-of-the-century fiction of Dreiser, Crane, and Norris and later in its influence upon such disparate figures as Dos Passos, Hemingway, and Faulkner, American literary naturalism has always been an elusive concept, quite capable of appropriating whatever it needed from realism, romanticism, or virtually any other -ism. Again, Charles C. Walcutt, in *American Literary Naturalism*, has discussed this protean nature of the tradition most thoroughly and convincingly. And Donald Pizer, in *Twentieth Century American Literary Naturalism*, recognizes the dynamic nature of naturalism. Focusing upon the fiction of Norman Mailer, Saul Bellow, and William Styron, Pizer investigates a new surrealistic naturalism that emphasizes individual character rather than social groups. Because American naturalism was, from the first, dynamic rather than static, it should not be surprising that as the twentieth century evolved and writers attuned to new ideas emerged naturalists began to incorporate key precepts of modernism, Sartrian existentialism, and the absurd. The result of such a dramatic merger was a new kind of fiction which Dreiser, for instance, might not have recognized, but one which Nelson Algren perfected. George Bluestone, perhaps the most sensitive of Algren's critics, insists that Algren is in fact not a naturalist ("Nelson Algren"). It would be more accurate to say that especially in the major phase of his career the novelist was engaged, as June Howard (1985) says, in *re*inventing naturalism.

Finally, while one must agree that Barth-Barthelme-Pynchon metafiction is one valid response to the cosmic dread of contemporary man, it is not the only one. An art which surrenders naive faith in scientific causality through recognition of existential anguish and the absurdity of material existence, but which retains a recognizably human (often even a specifically historical) setting, can still tell us much about the human condition. We know, after all, that certain historical events did occur, and we know that peculiarly human experiences are still applicable to each of us. World War II happened; the Great Depression of the 1930s happened; drug addiction is a fact. It is true that much of what happens to the world and to us seems inexplicable. Still, it is arguable that a writer such as Algren who portrays often inexplicable events happening to recognizably human characters in recognizably human environments can provide us with much aesthetic truth and comfort.

Algren was disturbed by the critical animosity toward and neglect of his work. His introduction to his 1947 short story collection, *The Neon Wilderness,* is part emotional defense of socially committed American writers—"the prevailing passion of American letters from Whitman through Crane to Steinbeck and Richard Wright" (10) and part invective against the postwar literary conquest of "Leslie Fleacure," "Justin Poodlespitz," and "footnote fellows" (10–13). While one must be aware of the presence in this polemic of the street-smart, intellectually naive persona Algren carefully cultivated, it is clear that he feared the demise of fiction committed to a realistic exploration of external reality. His subsequent work makes it clear that his fear arose less from the pronouncements of Fiedler and Podhoretz than from his own misgivings. Dreiser, Crane, and Kuprin, the Russian proponent of literary shock-effect calculated to produce social reform, are the main influences on Algren's first two novels, *Somebody in Boots* (1935) and *Never Come Morning* (1942). In *The Man With the Golden Arm,* however, Frankie Machine suffers at least as much from a crippling internal dread as he does from social injustice. Drug addiction, in fact, works as a unifying metaphor or trope for both Frankie's internal anxiety and the socioeconomic system which relentlessly oppresses him. At the conclusion of her translation of Sartre's *Being and Nothingness,* Hazel E. Barnes provides an appendix to the volume's terminology derived exclusively from the author's original language. In it, *anguish* is defined as:

> The reflective apprehension of the Self as freedom, the realization that a nothingness slips in between my Self and my past and future so that nothing relieves me from the necessity of continually choosing myself and nothing guarantees the validity of the values which I choose. Fear is of something in the world, anguish is anguish before myself (as in Kierkegaard). (799–800)

There is indeed much in Frankie's external world to fear. He is so much a victim of social injustice that his principle oppressors are hidden from him. It cannot be ignored, however, that Frankie is confronting an internal horror as well. The freedom to which Sartre's existential man is condemned is an unending sentence of choosing abstract values in a material and inherently valueless world. Throughout *The Man With the Golden Arm,* Frankie Machine attempts to flee a past in which he consistently avoided ethical choice and consequently plunged himself and others into a daily ritual of tedious suffering. He seeks literal and figurative prisons in which he can hide from the meaninglessness of his existence and the nothingness which has destroyed his 'Self.' Frankie is ultimately destroyed by his own anguish at the constant challenge of existential freedom, and no social reform movement could save him. In fact, Algren's belief in the efficacy of literary protest to produce social change was never complete, and by 1949 he was struggling to maintain some vestige of this idealistic faith. His much-celebrated compassion never deserted him, of course.

After *The Man With the Golden Arm,* Algren did not publish another novel for seven years, and when he did it was "accidental." At the request of his publishers he began revising *Somebody in Boots* for republication. Embarrassed by his first novel, he began rewriting it and ultimately produced an entirely different novel, *A Walk on the Wild Side.* A comparison of these two novels gives a clear indication of the metamorphosis which Algren's compassion had undergone. *Somebody in Boots* is sentimental in several ways, but most of all in its central depiction of unfeeling society which destroys helpless victims. Although Algren's faith in the efficacy of literary protest is not complete even here, the novel seems to have been primarily inspired by Marx, Dreiser, and Kuprin. The horror is largely environmental. In contrast, *A Walk on the Wild Side* emerges from an increasing cynicism; its mode is satire and its primary inspiration Céline.

In an interview, Algren expressed admiration for the "harsh compassion" of Edward Albee (Donohue 231–33), and nowhere is his own harshness so obvious as in *A Walk on the Wild Side.* The compassion which dominates *The Man With the Golden Arm* is an idiosyncratic blending of the Sartrian concepts of individual 'anguish'—which is a result of existential 'freedom'—and 'commitment.' In *Walk,* the compassion is almost concealed in a brutal, though ultimately Céline-like, forgiving satire. For the Algren of 1956, the horror permeated everyone and everything; no one was a victim, everyone was a victim.

Then for two decades Algren abandoned the novel. The most profound level of artistic despair, after all, is silence. He continued to write, publishing three miscellanies of travel literature, social and literary criticism, personal reminiscence, and even some short fiction between 1963 and 1973. The most important of the three miscellanies is *Who Lost an American?* (1963). In it, Algren experimentally blends absurdist travelogue, satire of a depersonalized America, and reminiscence of his Chicago childhood. The result is a volume controlled by a formless form, a unity paradoxically emerging from Algren's apparent decision to avoid any appearance of unity.

It is revealing to compare *Who Lost an American?* to Norman Mailer's *Advertisements for Myself.* Like *Who Lost an American?,* Mailer's book originated in a crisis of confidence. In 1959 Mailer no longer felt certain about the viability of the realistic-naturalistic tradition in fiction or about his own ability to write meaningful novels. Yet, *Advertisements for Myself* was a liberating book—it was Mailer's initial experiment in establishing a new persona, "Norman Mailer," at the heart of his writing. From it, he was able to move on to his best work, *Armies of the Night,* which solved the problem of fiction's viability to record fact by convincingly merging fiction and fact into a new plane of reality, since critically labelled "faction." Had Algren's despair not been more profoundly personal than Mailer's, *Who Lost an American?* might have performed the same liberating function for Algren.

In a fascinating volume of interviews, *Conversations with Nelson Algren,* published the year after *Who Lost an American?,* Algren insists that he will not do "another big book." One has to "go all out" to write "a big book," he says and then adds: ". . . I no longer see any reason for going all out" (Donohue 285–87). While insisting that there is no "meaningful work outside of the arts," he denies the potential of art or anything else to change society (257–61). More crucially, Algren discusses his own "loss of innocence" when he became unable to believe that his work was "wanted." Without much success, the interviewer, H. E. F. Donohue, attempts to force Algren to explain his feeling:

DONOHUE: How do you know when your work is wanted?
ALGREN: You feel that.
DONOHUE: Are there any other indications besides your feelings?
ALGREN: Nobody's work is absolutely wanted. But the point is—do you believe it's wanted, or not?
DONOHUE: Do you believe your work is wanted?
ALGREN: No, no. I don't know. I certainly did then.
DONOHUE: When?
ALGREN: Oh, up until the time and for a short time after I finished that *Man With the Golden Arm.* The fact that it may not be wanted isn't important. The fact is you believe it. (145)

What follows is a circular argument obviously emanating from an embittered mind. He knows his work isn't wanted, he says, because of his failure to achieve the level of commercial success enjoyed by lesser writers. He still feels anger over Otto Preminger's financial dishonesty with him and over the aesthetic perversion of his work in the film version of *The Man With the Golden Arm.* Still, he insists, "There's no point in doing it [writing] for the money." But there is also no point in going all out if one's work isn't wanted, as he knows his is not (146–51).

Later in the interviews Algren becomes less personal in his analysis and begins to argue more convincingly. No one in America wants big books now, he asserts—the critics want safe, middle-class novels, and the reading public wants escape. The only truly significant big book to emerge in America since World War II is Joseph Heller's *Catch-22*, he says, though he expresses great hope for Terry Southern and Thomas Pynchon (Donohue 274–77). Algren saw that the old naturalistic novel of protest could not capture contemporary reality. The concepts of naturalism and of protest would have to undergo significant transformations to remain viable. Heller, he says, had contributed significantly to such a transformation; the naturalistic technique and social protest present in *Catch-22* are enclosed within a layer of existential absurdity.

Algren's despair was especially regrettable because of what it prevented him from realizing about the implications of his own work. He had anticipated Heller with *A Walk on the Wild Side* (Algren knew this but seemed hurt that most critics did not). There is no indication that he saw the potentialities inherent in his more drastic experiment in absurdist form, *Who Lost an American?* This quite remarkable book did not then mark the beginning of a new and rich period of creativity for Algren as *Advertisements for Myself* did for Mailer. The loss to American letters is significant; certainly "Nelson Algren" was potentially as fascinating a persona as "Norman Mailer."

The sometimes mock-heroic and sometimes merely heroic "Norman Mailer" of such Mailer nonfiction fiction as *Armies of the Night* evolves out of *Advertisements for Myself. Advertisements* contains columns which appeared originally in *The Village Voice,* previously uncollected short stories, interviews, and poetry. Most memorably, it contains "The White Negro," the essay in which Mailer advanced "the hipster" as existential hero. The hipster, he says, is one who cultivates the psychopath within the Self and lives solely for the gratification of the moment—thus, in a state of perpetual becoming. Cumulatively, in *Advertisements for Myself,* Mailer introduces his best creation, "Norman Mailer," who will evolve into existential prophet, willfully extreme critic of all intellectual orthodoxy and outrageous challenger of cultural and social norms. "Mailer" is a decidedly cerebral and unmistakably eastern creation. In contrast, "Nelson Algren" of the first section of *Who Lost an American?* originates in the midwestern and frontier traditions of the mock innocent, the apparently unsophisticated literalist potentially exploited by linguistically sophisticated easterners—on the surface, a grown-up Huck Finn at the mercy of the weary cynicism of New York City. In the remainder of the book, "Algren" undergoes a metamorphosis first into committed American writer visiting Simone de Beauvoir and other existentialist friends in Europe and then into a nostalgic, but profoundly outraged, moral critic of Chicago. Despite these sharp differences, "Mailer" of *Advertisements for Myself* and "Algren" of

Who Lost an American? are both spontaneous characterizations evolving out of their creators' personal frustrations, cultural explorations, and intellectual probings. It is ironic and significant that Algren, in *Who Lost an American?*, refused to see Mailer as anything more than a "performer" and special favorite of a corrupt eastern literary establishment.

In the late fifties, throughout the sixties, and well into the seventies, the horror for Algren was something less tangible and more debilitating than socioeconomic injustice or even Sartre's anguish. It was perhaps the worst terror a novelist can confront: loss of faith in the value of one's own work and of fiction in general. Such a profound despair could not be overcome quickly or easily. It is not surprising then that his last novel did not begin as a novel. In the context of Algren's total career, it is fitting that it was inspired by apparent social injustice. In 1974 Algren left Chicago, the city with which he will always be most associated, for Paterson, New Jersey, to investigate the murder case against boxer Rubin "Hurricane" Carter. The state's case against Carter appeared shaky at best, and Algren believed the black boxer to be a classic victim of racial injustice. His belief was intensified by the atmosphere he discovered in Paterson. Ultimately, Algren moved to Sag Harbor on Long Island, largely to escape the vilification that descended upon him as a defender of Carter. In "Algren in Exile," the cover article in the February 1988 *Chicago* magazine, Joe Pintauro described Algren's bitterness and alienation while living on Long Island. Though at the end supported emotionally, professionally and sometimes financially by old friends including Gloria Jones, Kurt Vonnegut, and Pintauro himself, Algren never forgave the literary establishment for the critical and popular neglect which plagued his career.

More importantly, the originally conceived nonfictional investigation of the case underwent a considerable transformation. Herbert Mitgang reports in the foreword to *The Devil's Stocking* that Algren came to perceive the work as a novel instead of "reportage" because of fiction's "turnaround room" (4). At any rate, the Carter investigation became Algren's last novel, *The Devil's Stocking*. Despite changing the names of the key figures (Carter becomes Ruby Calhoun) and inventing a fictional prostitute as a unifying character, Algren produced a work close in form to such nonfiction fiction as Truman Capote's *In Cold Blood* and Mailer's *Executioner's Song*. Algren's book reads like a highly polished and controlled documentary. Like Capote and Mailer, Algren discovered that one method of controlling the confusing, contradictory flux of contemporary reality is to thoroughly depict an isolated aspect of that reality. In form, *The Devil's Stocking* marks yet another evolution of Algren's fiction. In theme, however, it represents a turning back. Undeniably a victim of society, Ruby

Calhoun still exhibits the kind of existential anguish that destroys Frankie Machine—the horror returns to the stage on which the man with the golden arm suffers and dies.

Despite his limited output, Nelson Algren deserves a closer critical examination than he has yet received. Because of the evolution in their form and content, his novels have a special interest for the student of contemporary American literature. He saw the need for and incorporated into his fiction significant modifications of the naturalistic tradition. He went far enough in this direction to be regarded as a significant novelist in his own right and to play a key role in the evolution of a contemporary or latter-day naturalism. It is a considerable journey from the episodic protest of *Somebody in Boots* to the absurdist satire of *A Walk on the Wild Side* and *Who Lost an American?*

2

Algren and the Crisis of Naturalism

*O*ne of the most eloquent statements of the contemporary novelist's despair at capturing the chaotic essence of post–World War II reality is Philip Roth's 1961 essay, "Writing American Fiction." Roth recounts the improbable details of the murders of two teenage girls in Chicago and the even more improbable media coverage of the events. All the survivors, including the mother of the girls and their killer, were transformed into celebrities, while the girls themselves were virtually forgotten. Any sense of tragedy and all awareness of horror were drowned in the flood of television and newspaper coverage. A despairing Roth then writes: "And what is the moral of so long a story? Simply this: that the American writer in the middle of the 20th century has his hands full in trying to understand, and then describe, and then make *credible* much of the American reality. It stupefies, it sickens, it infuriates and finally it is even a kind of embarrassment to one's own meager imagination" (144).

The implications of this feeling—which is increasingly widespread among contemporary American writers—for the realistic-naturalistic tradition are indeed ominous. How does one practice realism when reality is unreal and its unreality is heightened by a torrent of often irrelevant and even contradictory, information emanating from the media? Whatever else is implied by the term *literary naturalism*, it has traditionally rested upon two key assumptions: that it is capable of discovering an objectively verifiable truth and that human actions are, at least in part, determined by heredity, environment, and other external forces. Clearly, when reality becomes unreal, objective truth is an illusion and faith in external causality a mirage.

In an essay published seven years prior to Roth's, Maxwell Geismar, long an exponent of naturalism and an early advocate of Algren, expressed dismay over "The 'End' of Naturalism." The importance of Geismar's essay for this study is threefold: he emphasizes the historical capacity of American naturalism to incorporate the ideas of such diverse thinkers as Zola, Marx, and Nietzsche; he asserts that it has, except during the 1920s, been linked with "the demand for social reform"; and he recommends that young American writers look to such Europeans as Sartre, Camus, Moravia, Silone, and Cela for the inspiration necessary to reinvigorate the naturalistic tradition. What is especially valuable about Geismar's analysis is his understanding of the historically dynamic nature of American naturalism—his realization that the movement never was and need never be static and limited (*American Moderns* 20–27).

It is ironic, then, that in "Nelson Algren: *The Iron Sanctuary,*" an essay on Algren published four years later in 1958, Geismar is dismayed by *A Walk on the Wild Side:* "The tone of the book is no longer that of the Marxist morality which Algren shared with other writers in the 1930s, but often of ludicrous and demented farce" (*American Moderns* 192–93). Actually, Algren had not shared such a morality since his first novel, *Somebody in Boots.* Algren had, in fact, done precisely what Geismar recommended in "The 'End' of Naturalism"—he had turned to Europe, and specificially to Sartre and Céline, for a newer literary morality. As a result, he had created in *The Man With the Golden Arm* a strikingly different kind of naturalism. The extent to which *Walk* disturbed Geismar can be seen in a question he asks at the end of his essay: "Is this the end of the whole tradition of social protest which, as we have seen, Algren has embodied in his previous work and career?" (193). Algren had been Geismar's last major hope for the continuation of social protest, which the critic saw as essential to the tradition of realism. When he wrote *The Man With the Golden Arm,* Algren had already lost faith in the reformist potential of art. That loss did not mean, however, that he felt it necessary to abandon the lower classes who were, except in *Who Lost an American?,* always the subject and inspiration of his fiction. The novelist's commitment to slum dwellers survived his loss of faith in the possibility of changing their condition.

One of the earliest epitaphs for naturalism was Philip Rahv's 1949 essay, "Notes on the Decline of Naturalism." Rahv makes the important points that there never was a "pure" naturalist (not even Zola) and that it is necessary to separate naturalistic theory and practice. Zola and his American disciples such as Theodore Dreiser and Frank Norris called for scientific objectivity but never attained it. Zola cares for the economic victims in *Germinal;* Dreiser gives Carrie Meeber romanticism and sensitivity; and Norris treats McTeague with compassion, permitting him to return to his natural home among the miners before he dies. Rahv also suggests that even if reality is becoming unreal it can still be documented through a blending of the realistic tradition with Kafka-esque surrealism.

Like Geismar, Rahv seems to be exhibiting a sense of the dynamic nature of the naturalistic tradition. He certainly understands the difficulty of defining an aesthetic theory practiced by individuals as disparate as Dreiser, Crane, Norris, and Jack London. If one also considers Hemingway, Dos Passos, and Faulkner naturalists, the difficulty becomes severe. Thus, Rahv's concept of naturalism is a limited one:

> I would classify as naturalistic that type of realism in which the individual is portrayed not merely as subordinate to his background but as wholly determined by it—that type of realism, in other words, in which the environment displaces its inhabitants in the role of the hero. Theodore Dreiser, for example, comes as close as any American writer to plotting the careers of his characters strictly within a determinative process. (31)

An absolute determinism serves Rahv as social protest does Geismar—it is the single distinguishing characteristic of naturalism.

Abruptly, one realizes that Rahv does not, after all, see the tradition as an exceptionally dynamic one. When he insists that social determinism must be total, he rules out the possibility in a naturalistic work of environmental forces merging with an internal horror resulting from the necessity to make ethical choices in a chaotic, materialist universe.

One is not surprised when Rahv ends his essay by pronouncing naturalism's demise:

> And from a social-historical point of view this much can be said, that naturalism cannot hope to survive the world of nineteenth-century science and industry of which it is the product. For what is the crisis of reality in contemporary art if not at bottom the crisis of the dissolution of this familiar world? Naturalism, which exhausted itself in taking an inventory of this world while it was still relatively stable, cannot possibly do justice to the phenomena of its disruption. (37)

In this pronouncement, Rahv makes an assumption about the requisite technique, rather than the philosophy, of naturalism. The assumption is hardly a surprising one, given his nomination of Theodore Dreiser as the writer closest to "pure" naturalism. If external environment exercises a control so total as to become the hero of fiction, then it is logical that the novelist should thoroughly document it—just as Dreiser did.

Yet the degree to which the turn-of-the-century naturalists documented physical detail varied significantly. Dreiser and Frank Norris did believe that elaborate identification of minutia was essential to the evocation of fictional worlds—thus, Dreiser's detailed descriptions of Carrie Meeber's various living quarters and Norris's exhaustive naming of dental equipment in *McTeague*. Stephen Crane, in contrast, often utilizes recurrent patterns of symbolism, especially those emphasizing sharply contrasting colors, and linguistic irony to convey a sense of setting. This stylistic device has led some critics to argue that Crane was an "impressionist" rather than a naturalist. And, even in the novels written before *A Walk on the Wild Side,* Nelson Algren also avoids excessive detail. For Algren, ironic lyricism and grotesque humor substitute for documentation. One might assume then that Rahv, like George Bluestone, would insist that Algren is not a naturalist. Given the acknowledged contributions of such a lyrical symbolist as Crane to the naturalistic tradition, it makes more sense to say that Rahv defines the tradition too narrowly. Algren demonstrates in *The Man With the Golden Arm* that naturalism can accommodate external *and internal* forces of destruction.

Rahv's assertion that the chaos of post–World War II America cannot be conveyed through Dreiserian naturalism is valid. He is incorrect, however, in assuming that Dreiser's is the only conceivable naturalism. Even more clearly than Geismar, Algren understood that the tradition might continue to incorporate diverse and contradictory influences. He realized the dynamic nature of naturalism: Dreiser, Crane, Norris, and London responded to Zola, Nietzsche, Marx, and Rudyard Kipling; Algren drew inspiration from Dreiser, Crane, Kuprin, Sartre, and Céline.

Recent critical studies have focused on the historical and sociological forces which gave rise to naturalism as literary genre. In "American Literary Naturalism: The French Connection," Richard Lehan asserts that the rise of literary naturalism in France "cannot be divorced from a historical process that saw the movement from a landed to an urban economy, saw the rise of the bourgeoisie and at least the appearance of republican government, and that was ultimately founded on empirical/scientific assumptions about reality which, coupled with the new technology and power of money (new banks and credit theories), led to the impulse of nationalism and the rise of empire" (530). After discussing Zola's exhaustive attempt to document in fiction this dimension of French literary naturalism, Lehan points out that "the aftermath of the Civil War in America parallels the kind of historical changes taking place in France between 1848 and 1870 as both economies moved from a landed to a commercial/industrial world. In America this period witnessed the rapid growth of cities, the rise of corporate businesses, the influx of immigrant labor, and the practice of wretched working conditions" (545). According to Lehan, naturalism as literary genre must be seen as a purely historical phenomenon. It was, he believes, supplanted by modernism when "the generation of T. S. Eliot, Ezra Pound, James Joyce, and Virginia Woolf rejected the scientific basis of naturalism" and "replaced the mechanistic assumptions of naturalism with the more organic elements of symbolism and myth, relying on a human consciousness and theory of time mainly derived from Henri Bergson." After World War II, he concludes, "literary naturalism was all but dead," and "the world of Zola gave way to that of Thomas Pynchon" (556–57).

In her 1985 book, *Form and History in American Literary Naturalism,* June Howard also emphasizes the historical and socioeconomic conditions which produced American literary naturalism. Like Lehan, she views the late nineteenth-century urbanization of America as a central factor in the emergence of the genre. Urbanization was accompanied by "the greatest volume of immigration ever recorded," she writes; "in 1880, 80 percent of the population of New York was foreign-born or born of immigrants; in Chicago the figure was 87 percent; in Detroit 84 percent; in St. Louis and San Francisco, 78 percent" (33). A new "foreign" urban proletariat thus emerged in America.

Howard is especially perceptive in her analysis of the importance of point of view in turn-of-the-century American literary naturalism. The American naturalists were responding to a society characterized by an "omnipresent class conflict" (ix–x); and, just as for all fiction, an established, homogenized middle class constituted the dominant readership for their books. This middle-class readership inevitably saw the new foreign city dweller as a source of danger. Howard points out that "any study of late nineteenth-century and early twentieth-century America encounters . . . the sense . . . that there is an immediate threat to social order, a sense that the very foundations of American life are endangered." As a consequence, the turn-of-the-century reading public felt an urgent need to comprehend "the increasingly visible and largely immigrant industrial proletariat living in the cities" (75). Yet Howard also argues persuasively that the middle-class fascination with the new urban proletariat resulted from more than a need to comprehend. She utilizes Sartre's concept of projection of the Other to explain the full complexity of this fascination. The foreign city dweller became the evil Other for the homogenized middle class. Middle-class fears of uncontrolled and abnormal sexuality, of fail-

15

ure, of latent violence were projected onto this new and "unassimilated" urban American. Thus, for the middle class, the "terrain" of the urban proletariat took on an "exotic" aspect; and "like the anthropologist, the naturalist ventures into an exotic land to bring back reports on the savage inhabitants" (140). The various landscapes of the "savage" proletariat become "internal colonies" about which the naturalist, functioning as social scientist, reports to the civilized middle class (173).

Reflecting this fascination with a savage Other, turn-of-the-century American literary naturalism, Howard argues, is obsessed with the concepts of "the brute within" and "proletarianization." A character like Frank Norris's McTeague illustrates the capacity for animalism of which a savage urban dweller, devoid of civilizing reason, is capable. McTeague's decline into brutality is, of course, inspired by his sexuality (Howard 91). In *Vandover and the Brute,* Norris explored, with no little hysteria, the possibility that a member of the "civilized" middle class might degenerate into animalism. Dreiser's Hurstwood exemplifies a comparable nightmare— that such a character might descend into and be swallowed up by the terrain of the urban proletariat. Hurstwood's destruction is initiated by his sexual response to Carrie Meeber. Point of view again is crucial. Turn-of-the-century naturalists like Norris and Dreiser, Howard perceives, employed a narrative strategy fashioned after Sartre's " 'regard,' the look that denies reciprocity": they share with the reader a view of their characters as "objects rather than . . . self-aware subjects . . ." (150).

Like Lehan, Howard believes that the kind of fiction produced by Norris, Crane, Dreiser, and London must be seen as a historical phenomenon. Still, in discussing James T. Farrell's *Studs Lonigan* trilogy (1932–35) and Hubert Selby's *Last Exit to Brooklyn* (1964), she asks for critical consideration of a genre of latter-day naturalism (165–66). In discussing Selby's book, she offers another perceptive insight into point of view: here, "the narrator's voice is almost entirely merged with the characters" (165). Howard does not develop this insight, but it seems crucial to an understanding of the body of literature which might indeed be described as latter-day naturalism and to which Nelson Algren made a major contribution.

After the ascendancy of literary modernism, writers concerned with the urban lower classes no longer depicted central characters passively controlled by scientific external forces and primitive internal drives. Such writers as Selby, John Rechy, Joyce Carol Oates, and William Kennedy are central to June Howard's *"re*invention" of naturalism, which "serves new purposes" (166). These latter-day or contemporary naturalists, like their turn-of-the-century predecessors, focus on "them," the inhabitants of America's socioeconomic and psychological ghettos. The terrains depicted in their novels are inhabited by individuals foreign to the civilized middle-class reader. Like Norris and Dreiser, latter-day naturalists focus on and often document the victimization of their characters by the prevailing socio-economic structure. In a more profound way than Norris and Dreiser could be, they are also concerned with exploring the psychological effects of their characters' victimization. A shift in point of view, which is related to an overall narrative strategy, makes such psychological exploration possible. In the fiction of Selby, Rechy, Oates, and Kennedy, as in Algren's, narrative voice seeks identification with the victimized characters. Sartrian regard is abandoned in favor of a narration based precisely on reciprocity, an acknowledgment of the undeniable humanness of the urban lower classes.

Latter-day or contemporary naturalists incorporate central ingredients of modernism, especially an emphasis upon ambiguity and complexity of motivation. The suffering of their characters is not the result of such scientific factors as inherited alcoholism or avarice or poisons in the blood. McTeague and Hurstwood are supplanted by characters as psychologically complex as Jules Wendall of Joyce Carol Oates's *them* (1969), an intensely romantic young man who fears that he is "growing up into a man like every other man . . . [with] no destiny in proportion to his desire" (349). Psychological complexity and ambiguity of motivation do not, however, protect the contemporary naturalistic character from being overwhelmed by the physical, by sheer materiality. A vision of the absurdity of physical existence is central to such novels as *Last Exit to Brooklyn, them,* and John Rechy's *City of Night* (1963).

No writer played a more important role in the development of latter-day naturalism than Nelson Algren. In his fiction, narrative voice so identifies with character that the humanness of the middle-class reader is called into question. Yet some of the qualities which distinguish Algren's work led one critic to conclude that he was not a naturalist at all.

Because George Bluestone is the most perceptive Algren critic, his assertion that the novelist is not a naturalist merits specific attention. Bluestone argues that Algren "moves in the world of Dreiser, Farrell and Richard Wright" but insists that the novelist's "sensibility is his own." This sensibility, Bluestone says, is most clearly revealed in Algren's "curious disjuncture between conventional setting and offbeat prose" (27).

Bluestone's point seems to be that, while Algren writes about the lower depths of society familiar to students of American literary naturalism since *Maggie: A Girl of the Streets, McTeague,* and the account of Hurstwood's deterioration in *Sister Carrie,* he does not write about them in a naturalistic way. In effect, Algren depicts the world of his lumpenproletariat characters differently than did Dreiser, Crane, and Norris. Algren agreed with this evaluation. In interviews, he frequently stated his admiration for Dreiser but stressed that it was a limited kind of admiration. While comparing his work to James T. Farrell's, Algren once said: "Farrell is stenographic, and he isn't even a real good stenographer. He's too sloppy. In his essays he compares himself with Dreiser, but I don't think he's in Dreiser's league. He's as *bad* a writer as Dreiser . . . but he doesn't have the compassion that makes Dreiser's bad writing important" (Anderson and Southern 47). In fact, Algren consistently stressed his disappointment with such contemporary stenographic writers as Willard Motley.

In part, Bluestone's assertion of Algren's distance from naturalism rests upon the same assumption that causes Rahv to proclaim the movement's demise—the necessary relationship between naturalism as aesthetic theory and documentation as literary technique. While the fallacy of that assumption has been discussed, the fact that Stephen Crane avoided documentation is worth repeating. Not surprisingly, Algren's admiration for Crane was strong. He said once: "I'm not conscious of having my work shaped for me, but I'm sure Stephen Crane had something to do with where my interests in writing lie" (Corrington 132). Martha Heasley Cox and Wayne Chatterton's perceptive book on Algren contains an excellent discussion of the novelist's utilization of Crane's kind of impressionism instead of Zola-Dreiser documentation (72–73).

A related reason for Bluestone's separation of Algren from naturalism is the novelist's utilization of grotesque comedy. As often noted, *The Man With the Golden Arm* and *A Walk on the Wild Side* contain outrageous characters and scenes. The comedy in the latter work is part of what so disturbed Maxwell Geismar. Indeed, Algren's comedy is significantly different from the irony generally associated with naturalism. The difference originates in authorial attitude and is related to Algren's celebrated compassion. A comparison of *The Man With the Golden Arm*, Crane's *Maggie*, and Norris's *McTeague* will help to clarify this point.

There are things to laugh at in *McTeague*, especially the celebrated theater-going scene. As part of his awkward courtship of Trina, McTeague takes her, Mrs. Sieppe, and "little Owgooste" to a burlesque show. Norris has great fun belittling the primitive nature of the acts and the simplistic reactions of McTeague and his party to them. The scene, of course, ends with the debacle of little Owgooste wetting his pants. The scene is amusing, but in an unsettling way because one senses Norris's ridicule of the excruciatingly bad taste of his characters. This ridicule is a result of *McTeague's* narrative strategy. McTeague and the Sieppes are presented through a narrative focus which denies them reciprocity—they are the Other, the brute within, and the unassimilated immigrants to which the turn-of-the-century middle-class reader responded with fascination and horror.

There is a comparable scene in Crane's *Maggie: A Girl of the Streets,* in which Pete takes Maggie to a "show." The acts are every bit as ludicrous as those in *McTeague,* and Pete and Maggie are as impressed by them as are McTeague and his party. Still, largely because the scene is only three pages long and the writing impressionistic rather than satiric, one doesn't feel an authorial presence mocking the characters. Crane does not document and, more importantly, does not deny Maggie's humanness.

Algren's comedy is even more compassionate than Crane's restrained irony though its sources are often more grotesque than anything in either *McTeague* or *Maggie.* It is close to the comedy one finds in Céline—forgiving and accepting laughter at absurd individuals simply because despite their wretchedness they are, after all, human, alive. Céline and Algren considered the men and women of the lower classes capable of the most disgusting acts, but acts that only made manifest their humanness. In them, narrative focus identified with character. In his analysis of Algren in *Fiction of the Forties,* Chester E. Eisinger virtually dismisses Algren's capacity for ideas, asserting that the novelist never moved beyond an "impressionistic" Marxism. Eisinger is, however, perceptive in his analysis of Algren's compassion: "What distinguishes him is the way he blends his naturalism. He blends its determinism with a sympathy for his people that nevertheless cannot deter him from sending them to their miserable fates. And he blends a determinism which should rob them of will with an assertion of will—the will to love, the will to penance, the will to find the self—which testifies finally to their humanity." Eisinger points out that a key ingredient in this blend is Algren's sense of grotesque, yet embracing, comedy (84–85).

Algren then does not document (Eisinger claims that his "distinction" lies in the fact that "he is a naturalist who cares about style" [85]); his emphasis on environmental determinism was never complete and is least evident in his best books; and he perfected a kind of comedy foreign to the tradition. His faith in social protest as a viable means of achieving change was short-lived. One then has the choice between denying, along with Bluestone, Algren's connection with naturalism or, more accurately, suggesting that Algren contributed to the evolution of a latter-day or contemporary naturalism.

Bluestone's assertion that Algren uses a conventional setting is perceptive. Algren always wrote about the lumpenproletariat and is generally viewed as an urban novelist. Indeed, Blanche H. Gelfant, in *The American City Novel,* describes him as a leading practitioner of "the ecological novel," which "is distinguished from both the portrait and the synoptic novels by its reduction to a small spatial unit within the city" (12–13). In *Never Come Morning* and *The Man With the Golden Arm,* Algren takes a lower-class Polish-American section of Chicago as his exclusive subject—a significant contrast to John Dos Passos's *Manhattan Transfer,* whose protagonist is all of Manhattan (188). Gelfant's point is well taken: much of the power of both *Never Come Morning* and *The Man With the Golden Arm* originates in Algren's unrelenting focus upon the Chicago slums. A unique claustrophobic tone results from this emphasis; the reader feels that no world other than that of Lefty Bicek and Frankie Machine exists because, in actuality, none does for these characters. By denying any reality external to this one section of a large, impersonal city, Algren conveys Bicek's and Machine's entrapment. This kind of claustrophobic setting is perfected and carried to its logical extreme by Selby in *Last Exit to Brooklyn.*

Clearly, there is a connection between utilization of claustrophobic setting and environmental determinism. If there is no world outside it, any section of a city (however small or economically poor) has enormous power to control its inhabitants. Yet, Gelfant correctly senses that environment is not the sole destroying power in *The Man With the Golden Arm.* After describing the novel as "the outstanding city novel of the last decade" (approximately 1945 to 1954), she argues that it attains its power through depiction of a "common background of disorder." In other words, "what has reduced the people of Algren's novel is not simply poverty. Rather it is some inexplicable, irrational destructive force loosed in the world, which drives people on to frenzied and unrelenting acts of self-destruction" (252–53). Gelfant correctly senses that this destructive force resides partially within Algren's characters. She is one of a handful of critics (others are Geismar, Eisinger, and Bluestone) who *almost* perceive the existential core of Algren's best work.

The urban setting is, nevertheless, an important ingredient in *The Man With the Golden Arm,* and Algren will always be viewed as a Chicago writer, even though only two of his five novels utilize Chicago as a primary setting. As Gelfant perceives, those two, along with the best stories in *The Neon Wilderness,* reflect a strongly urban sensibility. This sensibility is distinctly midwestern as well and is the basis of the Algren persona central to *Who Lost an American?* One variation of this persona is the apparently unread and unsophisticated, street-wise midwesterner, bewildered by the urbanity of New York. This mock innocent has his roots in the fiction of such midwestern writers as Mark Twain and Sherwood Anderson. Algren, in *Who Lost an American?* and in essays, gives this characterization a peculiarly Chicago accent, one echoed by Mike Royko among others.

Algren and Royko can, in fact, be seen as the two prime figures in the development of a contemporary Chicago comic style. Their comedy originates in a complex response, consisting almost equally of moral outrage and aesthetic admiration, at the sheer audacity of Chicago's unique brand of civic corruption.

Still, Algren's conventional setting was not restricted to Chicago or even the Midwest. While it ends in Chicago, *Somebody in Boots* is primarily centered in small-town southwest Texas and New Orleans. *A Walk on the Wild Side*, which began as a revision of *Boots*, drops the Chicago ending and thus focuses entirely upon Texas's Rio Grande Valley and the city of New Orleans. There is, or course, a biographical explanation for Algren's regional emphasis in these two novels. After graduating from the University of Illinois with a degree in journalism during the Depression, he went on the road to New Orleans and to southwest Texas. In both places, Algren had adventures which, for sheer improbability, rival several of the more colorful experiences of his characters.

Aesthetically, the Rio Grande Valley and New Orleans complement Algren's Chicago in an unusual way. In his remarkable prose-poem, *Chicago: City on the Make* (1951), Algren emphasizes Chicago's origins as a center for frontier hustlers and con men. In *A Walk on the Wild Side*, he depicts the Rio Grande Valley as representing the sterility and decay of America's frontier legacy. Several essays in *The Last Carousel* (1973) demonstrate a comparable view—Algren is especially effective in depicting Bonnie and Clyde, among other Depression outlaws, as pathetic anachronisms attempting to follow a frontier ethic after the frontier as an emblem of escape and freedom has vanished. While the residents of Algren's small-town Texas are related to the visionaries who founded Chicago, they will found nothing—their ambition has decayed into petty meanness and their vitality into racism and a cruel religious fundamentalism. Cass McKay in *Somebody in Boots* and Dove Linkhorn in *A Walk on the Wild Side* seem to be exceptions to this general pattern: Cass possesses sensitivity and compassion, while Dove is certainly a man of vitality. The absurd reality of Depression America will, however, turn the virtues of these two characters into dangerous liabilities.

Algren's personal experience provided him a unique, synchronic vision of the development of America. The Rio Grande Valley preserved a decadent stage of the frontier legacy long after its vitality had produced the phenomenon of Chicago. New Orleans functions as a middle level of this synchronic vision. Algren's New Orleans never seems as claustrophobic as his Chicago, essentially because his characters don't feel trapped while in New Orleans. They are, in fact, quite trapped, but they nevertheless retain the illusion that growth and escape are possible. No one in the Chicago novels retains such an illusion.

Algren's conventional setting is the lower depths—whether Chicago, the Rio Grande Valley, or New Orleans. His commitment is consistently to the lumpenproletariat, those who have fallen off the socioeconomic ladder. He writes about drug addicts, prostitutes, pimps, con men, and hustlers. In his review of *A Walk on the Wild Side*, Leslie Fiedler charged Algren with a perverse romanticism in this restricted focus, labelling the novelist "the bard of the stumblebum," devoted to a "morality" of "pure corn" (43–44). Algren, in turn, pointed out, in the introductions to *The Neon Wilderness* and *Notes from a Sea Diary: Hemingway All the Way* (1965), the elitist assumption behind Fiedler's (and Norman Podhoretz's) criticism of his work—that only the middle and upper classes are worthy of being written about. He frequently argued that the legitimate legacy of American literature, inspired by such figures as Whitman, Dreiser, and Crane and preserved in the twentieth century by Richard Wright, Tennessee Williams, and, most significantly, Ernest Hemingway, is a "radical" rebellion against society. The truly legitimate American writer, he asserts, must take a position outside of and in opposition to society. One way to claim such a position is to utilize a narrative strategy emphasizing reciprocity between narrative voice and socially despised characters.

Despite the eloquence with which Algren has often defended his radical position, one must grant that his commitment to the lower depths is, to a degree, romantic. He does not, Fiedler and Podhoretz to the contrary, romanticize his social outcasts. Still, he makes an inverted elitist assumption of his own. In contrast to Fiedler and Podhoretz, Algren asserts that the middle and upper classes are almost never worth writing about because they are hypocritical and dull. Further, the respectable elements in society prey upon the downtrodden—it is the middle class which most condemns prostitutes, he argues, and it is middle-class males who most frequently pay for their services.

An extended discussion of the Fiedler-Podhoretz and the Algren positions about socioeconomic class and the proper study of literature is beside the point here. Algren's commitment to the lumpenproletariat does, however, merit further discussion. Initially inspired by the economic suffering Algren experienced and observed during the Depression, it began as social protest, with its intellectual and artistic roots in Marx, Kuprin, and Dreiser. At this point, Algren believed in the potential of art to effect social change. When that faith began to dissipate, the novelist still maintained his loyalty to the lower classes, largely because of his sense of American literature's historic relationship to radicalism and his contempt for "respectability." His faith was then transformed into the harsh compassion of *A Walk on the Wild Side.*

However romantic, this commitment became increasingly existential. In *Conversations with Nelson Algren,* the novelist defines American literature:

> American literature is the woman in the courtroom who, finding herself undefended on a charge, asked, "Isn't anybody on my side?" It's also the phrase I used that was once used in court by a kid who, on being sentenced to death, said, "I knew I'd never get to be twenty-one anyhow." More recently I think American literature is also the fifteen-year-old who, after he had stabbed somebody, said, "Put me in the electric chair—my mother can watch me burn." Even *more* recently, American literature is a seventeen-year-old kid picked up on a double murder charge . . . who said he was very glad it happened, he had absolutely no regrets, his only fear was that he might not get the electric chair. . . . That's the only fear he has, that he might have to continue to live. . . . I think it's also the girl who says, "It don't matter what happens to me because it's really happening to somebody else. I'm not really here." I think American literature consists of these people. . . . (Donohue 278–81)

The shift in emphasis following the phrase "*more* recently" is revealing. Algren is acknowledging that his initial focus was on social victims such as the isolated prostitute in the hostile courtroom. At some point, his vision broadened to include more frightening victims (the young double murderer who fears only life) and the surreal (the girl who isn't "really here").

Whether prompted by social protest or a sense of existential absurdity, Algren's devotion to the lower depths is intended to challenge the reader in a way that the fiction of Norris and Dreiser could not. He was not concerned with anthropological explorations of internal colonies, but with shocking his middle-class readers into full recognition of the humanity of the outcast inhabitants of the lower depths. It is likely that a part of Algren's anger at Fiedler's and Podhoretz's attacks on his work was prompted by an awareness that these and other critics were determined to deny any such common bond with the lumpenproletariat.

Algren's conventional setting is an integral part of his dynamic naturalism. Even though his belief in environmental determinism was not as complete as theirs, he followed Dreiser, Crane, and Norris in his search for subject matter. Donald E. Pizer has written that "[Stephen] Crane, then, is a naturalistic writer in the sense that he believes that environment molds lives" ("*Maggie,*" 175). So long as a distinction is made between the words *molds* and *controls,* Pizer's assertion can be applied to Nelson Algren as well.

3

Algren's Influences: Kuprin, Sartre, and Céline

*T*he evolution of Algren's views concerning environment and external determinism can best be approached through a comparison of his work with that of Kuprin, Sartre, and Céline. In the interview acknowleding Stephen Crane's role in shaping his work, Algren adds, "and Alexander Kuprin." This follows a list of books which have influenced him, including Crane's *Maggie*, Kuprin's *Yama*, and Céline's *Journey to the End of the Night* (Corrington 132). When interviewed by the *Paris Review*, he first said that Dostoyevsky was the only Russian he had "re-read," but quickly added, "No, that ain't all, there's Kuprin" (Anderson and Southern 46). And, of course, he places the quotation from *Yama* concerning the horror on the opening page of *The Man With the Golden Arm*.

Initially, it seems strange to discover a contemporary novelist so strongly and directly influenced by *Yama*. It is even stranger to find that same writer praising Kuprin along with such existential writers as Céline and Dostoyevsky. At least in translation, *Yama, or The Pit* (1909, 1914, 1915) now reads more like an intensely sincere, if naive, tract against the evils of prostitution than a novel. It is more than episodic; it is inordinately digressive. Certainly, the novel's most modern aspect is the analysis of the horror of prostitution delivered by Platonov, a journalist utilized not very successfully by Kuprin as a unifying device, and partially quoted by Algren:

. . . horrible are the everyday accustomed trifles, these business-like, daily, commercial reckonings. This thousand year old science of amatory practice, this prosaic usage, determined by the ages. In these unnoticeable nothings are completely dissolved such feelings as resentment, humiliation, shame. There remains a dry profession, a contract, an agreement, a well-nigh honest petty trade, no better, no worse than, say, the trade in groceries. Do you understand, gentlemen, that all the horror is in just this, that there is no horror! Bourgeois work days— and that is all. And also an after taste of an exclusive educational institution, with its naiveté, harshness, sentimentality and imitativeness. (100–101)

Thus, the horror of prostitution, according to Platonov and, one assumes, Kuprin, is in society's prosaic acceptance of such a vicious form of dehumanization. The horror is that no one is particularly horrified—not even the victimized prostitutes themselves.

Platonov's speech is relevant to Algren's fiction in more than one way. One of the many oversimplifications in Norman Podhoretz's attack on *A Walk on the Wild Side* concerns Algren's treatment of prostitutes: ". . . these lovable creatures, endowed to a girl with childlike innocence, are in good standing, up to a point. If only they could live the wild life willingly without dreaming of chicken farms and children, they would be all right, but most of them feel victimized" (137). The central assumptions behind Podhoretz's evaluation are simply wrong: Algren does not approve of the exploitation of prostitutes, and he does not perceive them as lovable innocents. Their exploitation, he believes, is part of the larger societal exploitation of the lumpenproletariat; and he depicts them as brutalized *individual* women. As will be discussed later, Algren's treatment of prostitutes represents, especially in comparison to the sentimentality of a John Steinbeck, a complex experiment in narration.

Algren does assign a type of innocence to his prostitutes, but it does not originate in any simplistic heart-of-gold stereotype. Instead, it is the innocence implied in Platonov's analysis of the horror and emphasized by Kuprin throughout *Yama*. Of necessity, the prostitutes in Kuprin's novel have had to suppress, even deny, their full human complexity. Moreover, they are often treated as children by their exploiters and as a result have not developed into fully mature women. Kuprin describes the experience of one particular prostitute as being typical: "At fourteen years she was seduced, and at sixteen she became a patent prostitute, with a yellow ticket and a venereal disease. . . . And so her mental development, her experience, her interests, remain on an infantile plane until her weary death . . ." (134). If an unusually intelligent or sensitive girl rebels against this enforced infantilism, she is brutally beaten.

Nevertheless, a few of Kuprin's victimized women do rebel. A prostitute named Jennka contracts syphilis and then coldly plans to infect as many of her clients as possible. She knows exactly what she is contemplating: " 'A person rots ten, twenty, thirty years. Any second paralysis can strike him down, so that the right side of his face, the right arm, the right leg dies—it isn't a human being that's living, but some sort of a little half. Half-man— half-corpse. The majority of them go out of their minds . . .' " (352). Jennka's calculated plan to destroy those who use her foreshadows Algren's characterization of Kitty Twist in *A Walk on the Wild Side*. Kitty Twist is, in fact, much more ruthless and cynical than Jennka, who finally commits suicide instead of carrying out her revenge.

Algren found in Kuprin's depiction of prostitution a telling vision of prosaic, socially accepted, horror. He then transported this vision from czarist Russia to the twentieth-century United States. He generally accepted Kuprin's explanation of why so ancient an evil as prostitution continues to exist. Norman Podhoretz could hardly be more mistaken in his charge that Algren actually endorses "the wild life." Like Kuprin, Algren believed that prostitution, like all forms of vice, flourishes because hypocritical "decent" people want it to. In *Yama,* a prostitute named Tamara issues a challenge to some socially prominent visitors to the brothel: " 'We are fallen, but we don't lie and don't pretend, but you all fall, and lie to boot. Think it over for yourself; now—in whose favour is this difference?' " (205). Throughout his work, Algren attacked the American legal system for punishing individual prostitutes and drug addicts instead of seriously attempting to end either form of exploitation.

It is significant that he used the Kuprin quote about the "horror" in *The Man With the Golden Arm,* his only novel which does not deal to any important degree with prostitution. Kuprin helped Algren formulate a stance toward all social injustice. Human exploitation existed in modern America, he believed, because the middle and upper classes who control society's legal apparatus profited from it.

Such a view is, of course, overly simple; Algren, in fact, found in Kuprin a naive faith in the power of art to reform society. The journalist Platonov, speaking for his creator, delivers a prophecy in *Yama:*

. . . there will come a writer of genius, and precisely a Russian one who will absorb within himself all the burdens and all the abominations of this life and will cast them forth to us in the form of simple, fine, and deathlessly-caustic images. And we shall all say, "Why, now, we ourselves, have seen and known all this, but we could not even suppose that this is so horrible. . . ." (112)

Alexandre Kuprin was the Russian writer Platonov had in mind. To a point, Nelson Algren aspired to be his American counterpart.

Kuprin directly stated his belief in the power of art in an "Author's Postscript," which he wrote in 1929 for the Modern Library edition of *Yama*. This postscript is even more idealistic than the novel itself. Kuprin asserts that he is "deeply convinced of the fact that *Yama* has compelled many people to reflect, with sincere sympathy, about prostitution" (437); he then stresses his "rejoicing" over *Yama*'s American publication because "there, on a time, appeared *Uncle Tom's Cabin*" (442). *Yama*, he believed, might end prostitution just as Stowe's novel contributed to the abolition of slavery. Always aware that prostitution exists because respectable people desire it, Kuprin prescribes an extensive program of mental and physical hygiene aimed at helping young males to control their lust.

Until he began to see at least as much horror in existential absurdity as in economic injustice, Algren shared Kuprin's faith in the power of art to reform. His definition of American literature indicates, however, that he came to see the causes of suffering as being much more complex than indicated by the Kuprin of *Yama*. Mental and physical hygiene could not help the condemned seventeen-year-old boy seeking to escape life or the young girl who doesn't care what happens to her because she's "not really here."

Algren never admitted any influence upon his work by Sartre. On more than one occasion, in fact, he went to some pains to deny that Sartre's ideas had influenced him. Yet, he was Sartre's friend and had a celebrated love affair with Simone de Beauvoir. Moreover, Sartre admired Algren's work, and his translation of *Never Come Morning* was instrumental in the international success of Algren's second novel (Cox and Chatterton 110). Ultimately, the question of precise influence is not of great importance. What does matter is the fact that Algren gradually developed concepts of human freedom and the social function of literature which are comparable to key ideas of Sartre. It is then valid to discuss *The Man With the Golden Arm* in Sartrian language.

At first glance, literary naturalism and Sartrian existentialism might seem to be absolutely antithetical concepts. From the first, environmental determinism has been central to naturalism. Crane's Maggie, for example, is largely a helpless victim of her alcoholic mother and the corrupt urban environment of the Bowery. Throughout his career, Sartre emphasizes man's paradoxical freedom. The determinism of naturalism and the 'freedom' of Sartrian existentialism are not, however, as incompatible as they might initially appear.

A comparison of Sartre's abstract and largely nonpolitical 1943 philosophical investigation, *Being and Nothingness,* with his 1947 call for a literature of political 'commitment', *What is Literature?,* illustrates the way in which Sartre's ideology often underwent dramatic shifts. *Being and Nothingness,* which perhaps as much as any single work revolutionized the modern consciousness, is a formal academic dialectic. While its style is deliberately abstract and impersonal, its concern is with the nature of individual human freedom. *Being and Nothingness,* of course, first elaborated the crucial terminology of modern French existentialism: *Being-in-itself, being-for-itself, anguish, bad faith, commitment,* and *freedom.*

Being-in-itself (the *être-en-soi*) is defined as "non-conscious Being" (800); it is the base materiality into which man is born, existence as a corporeal entity subject to decay and death. In contrast, *being-for-itself* (the *être-pour-soi*) constitutes the "nihilation" of being-in-itself; it is "consciousness conceived as a lack of being, a desire for Being . . ." (800). Being-for-itself represents that "essence" toward which man must strive if he is to create a Self, but which, nevertheless, can never be quite realized. In his pioneering study of modern existentialism, *Irrational Man,* William Barrett describes the paradox of man's striving toward an "authentic" for-itself:

> Human existence is thus a perpetual self-transcendence; in existing we are always beyond ourselves. . . . Our existence from moment to moment is a perpetual flying beyond ourselves, or else a perpetual falling behind our possibilities; in any case, our being never exactly coincides with itself. It could do so only if we sank into the self-contained form of the being of a thing, and this would be possible only if we ceased to be conscious. (245)

There is in Sartre's universe an unending temptation for Western man to abandon the exhausting and ultimately hopeless attempt to create an authentic Self. This temptation takes several forms. Man is conceived in materiality and is perennially reminded of the base and transitory nature of matter (especially in its manifestation as flesh). Moreover, in the twentieth century, Western man lives in a society devoted to material possessions and increasingly controlled by technology. Thus, he cannot avoid yearning for the preconscious and self-contained state of "the thing." Frankie Machine's drug addiction in *The Man With the Golden Arm* functions as a metaphor for such an attempted return to the preconscious.

Bad faith is as elusive as any term in Sartre's special vocabulary. In Barnes's appendix to *Being and Nothingness,* the concept is described as "a lie to oneself within the unity of a single consciousness. Through bad faith a person seeks to escape the responsible freedom of Being-for-itself." In Sartre's philosophical treatise, bad faith represents the attempt to avoid the challenge of creating a responsible Self by striving for essence, or Being-for-itself. As unavoidable as this temptation is, it is ethically irresponsible since it constitutes a surrender to brute materiality. Sartre's *freedom* is, in fact, as harsh as it is ethically necessary: "Freedom. The very being of the For-itself which is 'condemned to be free' and must forever choose itself— i.e., make itself . . . success is not important to freedom" (803). While man cannot totally escape awareness of being-in-itself, he cannot yield to it without surrendering his authentic Self. To transcend nothingness, man must make a commitment to strive toward essence, being-for-itself. It is hardly surprising that the myth of Sisyphus is attractive to Albert Camus and other existentialists. Freedom, to them, means freedom to choose—to push toward an impossible goal—total self-definition or authenticity.

Having established the basic lexicon of his version of existentialism in *Being and Nothingness,* Sartre revised it throughout his career. In his excellent deconstructionist analysis, *A Preface to Sartre,* Dominick La Capra provides a clear and concise summary of the evolutions in the philosopher-novelist's thought. La Capra writes that

> Sartre's journey would be demarcated by radical conversions or identity crises that totalize his life or thought up to that point and provide the basis for a new original choice of being. . . . One crisis would come with World War II, when Sartre was jolted out of his apolitical individualism to discover History and the problem of commitment.

It would be more accurate to say that World War II, the Nazi occupation of France, and the Holocaust forced Sartre out of his intellectual abstraction and into a reexamination, and ultimately a redefinition, of commitment. *What is Literature?* was the immediate response of this "new Sartre."

Much of *What is Literature?* consists of Sartre's analysis of the limitations and failures of eighteenth- and nineteenth-century French literature. In the eighteenth century, he argues, the bourgeoisie captured literature and then proceeded to utilize it as a means of seeking truth about "universal man." Since only individual men exist, universal man is a fallacy, and eighteenth-century French literature is a quest for nonexistent truths about a nonexistent being. Yet, nineteenth-century French realism, especially as practiced by Flaubert, was for Sartre the ultimate betrayal of what literature should be. Flaubert and the nineteenth-century realists, he argues, practiced the supreme hypocrisy of pretending that they were not equally the captives of the bourgeoisie. In fact, they pretended disdain for the middle classes who were, of course, the very people who read them. Moreover, they expressed a total and sweeping contempt for the lower classes. Sartre argues that the inevitable result of this revolt against any restrictive audience was an irrelevant art for art's sake, in which the French writer addressed himself and attempted to communicate with no one else.

We are still so hampered by this legacy in the twentieth century, he argues, that we have not realized the necessity of a committed literature, "a literature of engagement." In a literature of engagement, the novelist seeks, above all, to bring about change: "The 'engaged' writer knows that words are actions. He knows that to reveal is to change and that one can reveal only by planning to change. He has given up the impossible dream of giving an important picture of Society and the human condition" (23). The specific change that the engaged writer should seek to bring about is a classless society: ". . . *actual* literature can only realize its full *essence* in a classless society" (156).

Sartre concludes *What is Literature?* by summarizing the key assumptions and goals of a literature of engagement. Emphasizing the difficulty of bringing about such a literature in the capitalist West, he presents, nevertheless, an outline of how it would ideally come about. First, the committed writer should address a "concrete universality," that is, "the sum total of men living in a given society." Above all, such an artist should not be "a clerk" consciously addressing only an elite circle (as Sartre accuses Flaubert of having been), for "a clerk is always on the side of the oppressors." A committed literature would, in fact, be an agent of "permanent revolution": it would be "a synthesis of Negativity, as a power of uprooting from the given, and a Project, as an outline of a future order." The engaged writer would address "a public which has the freedom of changing everything; which means, besides suppression of classes, abolition of all dictatorship, constant renewal of frameworks, and the continuous overthrowing of order once it begins to congeal" (155–59).

Clearly, Sartre moved from the isolated world of the academy into "history" between 1943 and 1947. In this journey, he took along, however, the essential vocabulary of *Being and Nothingness,* extending and amplifying key terminology—by 1947, the unending struggle for becoming had been extended to all society which the writer must help plunge into a state of permanent revolution against order or those recurrent ideologies which entrap man. Dominick La Capra offers a cogent account of how Sartre, throughout the remainder of his career, essentially extended the key assumptions of a committed or engaged literature. Still challenged by history (Vietnam, the Paris student revolt, etc.) and increasingly by a new French intellectual avant-garde led by Roland Barthes, he sought to "integrate" and "ultimately dissolve" existentialism within Marxism.

Despite Nelson Algren's occasional denials of any knowledge of existentialism, he was certainly aware of Sartre's brand of existentialism. In fact, he publicly took Sartre and Simone de Beauvoir's side in their 1954 debate with Albert Camus over the political responsibility of literature. It is, moreover, not difficult to relate Sartre's vision of engaged literature to Algren's concept of the radical legacy of American literature. Algren, in fact, did not need Sartre or anyone else to tell him that a writer must be committed to the oppressed and a foe of the oppressors and the systems of order which they repeatedly construct. From the beginning of his career, Algren was committed to the urban lumpenproletariat, society's despised rejects, and every bit as hostile to the bourgeoisie as Sartre. Even as he increasingly lost faith in the possibility of meaningful societal change, Algren's devotion to the urban outcast remained intact. He granted reciprocity to his lumpenproletariat characters while treating middle-class society with a variation of Sartrian regard.

In his best fiction, Algren, like other postwar writers, utilized Sartre's vision of modern man's struggle to create an authentic Self while trapped in materiality and the temporal to add complexity to his characters. Algren is not the only modern American writer whose work exhibits a merging of environmental determinism and elements of existentialism; one needs only to think of the fiction of Hemingway, Faulkner, and Dos Passos, among others. The origin of Sartrian freedom in Nietzsche's declaration of the death of God allows it a compatibility with environmental determinism. In Sartre's vision, man did not choose to be free, rather he was "condemned to be free" by the death of God and the subsequent entrapment in material existence. Sartrian choice and the possibility of essence come into play only after man has been sentenced to existence within time, decay, and death. Moreover, man is unique in his consciousness of the fate unavoidably awaiting him. Man's realization that there is "no exit" from materiality and time results in absurdity and "nausea." It is important to remember that Sartre's philosophy derived from Nietzsche's negation of the Christian existential legacy represented by Kierkegaard and Dostoyevsky. Consequently, some of Sartre's most severe critics have been twentieth-century Christian existentialists. For instance, Gabriel Marcel's essay, "Existence and Human Freedom," is a harsh repudiation of Sartre. Marcel writes that "Sartre himself constantly asserts that man is a useless passion. . . . Man's life is an attempt, continually renewed and inevitably doomed to failure, at the divinisation of himself. . . . [In Sartre] we are . . . in the presence of explicit and aggressive atheism" (*Philosophy* 84). Marcel's criticism is essentially accurate—for the individual man or woman, Sartrian freedom is the freedom to strive perennially and, in the last analysis, futilely to create an authentic Self.

Algren's professed devotion to Dostoyevsky to the contrary, his work also reveals an explicit and aggressive atheism. God has long been dead in Algren's world; religion is a meaningless ritual, a grim joke, or part of the overall system which exploits his characters. One reason that the existential aspect of Algren's work has been largely ignored may well be his devotion to the lumpenproletariat. His later theory to the contrary, Sartre is known for depicting in his fiction alienated intellectuals standing outside society— Roquenten in *Nausea,* for example. This kind of isolated character observing society from the outside, in fact, dominates modern existential fiction—the existential hero is typically the stranger. It is not difficult to see an affinity between the fictional creations of Sartre and Camus and the antiheroes of Hemingway, for instance. In contrast, Algren's "stumble-bums," petty criminals, and prostitutes are the rejects and victims of society. Their desperate socioeconomic status does not, however, necessarily exempt them from the internal struggle to create an authentic Self.

Algren's relationship to existentialism is, in fact, comparable to Richard Wright's. Both Algren and Wright, who were close friends, began as naturalistic exponents of social protest. Their work always contained, however, a sense of the absurd. In both cases, an emphasis upon existential absurdity ultimately dominated their devotion to protest. Wright's *The Outsider* is a very different kind of book than either *Black Boy, Native Son,* or *American Hunger* in much the same way that *The Man With the Golden Arm* is different from *Somebody in Boots* and *Never Come Morning.* Wright's loyalty to his race always remained intact, as did Algren's devotion to the lumpenproletariat. Yet both men experienced a profound disillusionment with Marxism and the possibility of social justice. Ironically, both began to develop personal associations with the Sartrian circle as Sartre was moving radically to the Left.

William Barrett argues that Sartre's novel, *Nausea,* was written out of a sense of "disgust," but he stresses that Sartre's disgust lacks "the grand scope and implications of Céline's" and that it is overly abstract, "not embodied as Céline's is, in the desperate picaresque of common life and the anonymous depths of street characters" (251). This evaluation seems accurate. It is, moreover, relevant to Algren's acknowledgement of Céline's influence upon his work. In addition to including *Journey to the End of the Night* in his list of memorable books, Algren once said that he had written in the tradition of Dreiser, Crane, and Céline (Donohue 195).

What Algren found in *Journey to the End of the Night* (1934) was a model for maintaining a harsh compassion while confronting the full scope and implications of human depravity. He discovered in Céline a cruel, but ultimately forgiving, mode of satire. Certainly, *Journey,* like *Death on the*

Installment Plan, is a harsh and brutal work. Episodic in structure, it recounts the adventures of one of modern literature's most memorable antiheroes, Bardamu, in World War I, French West Africa, New York City, Detroit, and Paris.

Everywhere, Bardamu encounters nothing but misery and suffering and decides that his vision must be communicated to the world:

> The biggest defeat in every department of life is to forget, especially the things that have done you in, and to die without realizing how far people can go in the way of crumminess. When the grave lies open before us, let's not try to be witty, but on the other hand, let's not forget, but make it our business to record the worst of the human viciousness we've seen without changing one word. When that's done, we can curl up our toes and sink into the pit. That's work enough for a lifetime. (18)

This vision of human crumminess and viciousness is the core of an aesthetic of hatred which dominates most of the novel. Moreover, wherever he is, Bardamu lives among the lower classes and sees them as exploited by a vicious class system. Céline's sense of human misery is based on both internal and external suffering.

Consciousness for Céline is merely an instrument of further torture because it heightens one's awareness of the inevitability of pain and death. Time and its ally, the material, have the same function in Céline's vision as in Sartre's early philosophy: they constitute the virtually inescapable absurdity of existence. What Barrett called "the grand scope" of Céline derives from the novelist's application of his disgust to the lumpenproletariat in particular and mankind in general: "Maybe, if people are so wicked, it's only because they suffer, but years can elapse between the time when they stop suffering and the time when their characters take a turn for the better" (61).

Bardamu's gradual realization of the complexity and universality of suffering enables him to move subtly away from pure hate toward forgiveness. In describing a trick played on tramps in New York City, he admits the existence of idealism: "You know about innards? The trick they play on tramps in this country? They stuff an old wallet with putrid chicken innards. Well, take it from me, a man is just like that, except that he's fatter and hungrier and can move around, and inside there's a dream" (168). In Detroit, Bardamu becomes infatuated with a prostitute and finds acceptance: "That was the first place in America where I was received without brutality, amicably in fact, for my five dollars" (195). One can imagine Algren responding to the description of Bardamu's brothel experience on two levels: he would appreciate the irony (the five dollars *is* required), and he would agree with the implication that only among the lumpenproletariat can one forge human relationships. Certainly, he would have accepted Céline's concept that class systems, especially in capitalistic nations, are based upon hatred. Thus, only the thoroughly oppressed can reach out to each other.

Bardamu's sense of a bond with the wretched increasingly becomes clearer: "Like my mother, I could never feel entirely innocent of any horrible thing that happened" (239). Bardamu is a man; men do horrible things; Bardamu cannot then condemn. (As will be discussed, Algren's police officer in *The Man With the Golden Arm,* Record Head Bednar, is profoundly shaken by a comparable epiphany during a police lineup.) Bardamu also comes to realize that, "crummy" as they are, people offer the only refuge from the world's misery: "A time comes when you're all alone, when you've come to the end of everything that can happen to you. It's the end of the world. Even grief, your own grief, doesn't answer you anymore, and you have to retrace your steps, to go back among people, it makes no difference who" (283). Céline's narrative strategy emphasizes the petty viciousness of his characters while utilizing a narrative voice which identifies with them. Their crumminess is documented as their humanness is affirmed. Animalistic behavior does not make these characters objects, they always remain self-aware subjects.

Yet people are only a refuge. There is no escape from time and matter, thus the consciousness of death: "Life is like that! That's how everything ends. In absurdity" (Céline 305). At one point, Bardamu experiences a night vision of all the dead, who vanish with the dawn. Like much of Céline, the passage is both lyrical and despairing. Bardamu accepts his brotherhood with the dead men obscured by the mist. Reality becomes surreal, and he surrenders to "the usual delirium of the world" (72).

Céline, like Kuprin, means for his art to shock, but his purpose is otherwise quite different. He is writing cosmic, not social, protest. The absurd cannot be reformed, but it can be resisted through the creation of art. To be honest, however, that art must acknowledge and record man's capacity for both petty and large-scale viciousness—and then accept and forgive. Since, in absurdity, existence ends for all, all are brothers and sisters. Perhaps the most revealing passage in all Céline stresses his concept of a reluctant human community:

> People have plenty of pity in them for the infirm and the blind, they really have love in reserve. I'd often sensed that love they have in reserve. There's an enormous lot of it, and no one can say different. But it's a shame that people should go

on being so crummy with so much love in reserve. It just doesn't come out, that's all. It's caught inside and there it stops, it doesn't do them a bit of good. They die of love—inside. (310)

Algren stressed the influence of Kuprin and Céline throughout his career; and, in reserve or not, his love for the economically exploited is always present. Still, his later, best work is dominated by existential anguish and absurdity more than the overt social protest of *Somebody in Boots*. As with most artists (as opposed to systematic philosophers like Sartre), Algren's thought is not characterized by dramatic shifts; rather, his emphasis evolved from novel to novel.

As mentioned, even though both *The Man With the Golden Arm* and *A Walk on the Wild Side* are illustrative of the central thesis of *Radical Innocence,* Ihab Hassan's 1961 study of post–World War II American fiction, it contains no mention of either novel by Algren. This exclusion is all the more surprising in that Hassan does discuss other generally neglected representations of "the unfound generation," including James Jones. In *Radical Innocence,* Hassan argues convincingly that our postwar fiction is dominated by a distinctly American version of modern existentialism.

To a large degree, existentialism became a major influence in American literary circles after the war for the essential reasons that it dominated European thought and literature. World War II and its immediate aftermath represented for large numbers of American intellectuals the death of several old, sustaining beliefs: Hiroshima and the Holocaust underscored the death of God more dramatically than any philosophical proclamation could have; Stalin's brand of totalitarianism made it difficult to retain the "old Left" faith in Marxism; and the acceleration of technology and bureaucracy dramatized the insignificance of the individual. Hassan concisely summarizes the effects of this new and alien universe on American novelists: "Obviously, a dark impulse of *resistance* permeates contemporary letters. . . . [American novelists] agree that the contemporary world presents a continued affront to man, and that his response must therefore be the response of the rebel or victim, living under the shadow of death. . . . The contemporary self recoils, *from* the world, *against* itself. It has discovered absurdity" (4–5). He adds that the point is really not that human existence in the contemporary world is any more desperate than it ever has been, but that our consciousness tells us it is (32). Again, in Sartre, it is modern man's *consciousness* of his entrapment in time and materiality which is his real curse. Our writers' "dark impulse of *resistance,*" their emphasis on the rebel and the victim, lead to their creation of the contemporary antihero as the focus of their work and to their extensive utilization of irony. The discrepancy between modern man's dreams and his potentiality makes irony the obvious mode of the contemporary existential novel. It is at least interesting to remember that, for not totally dissimilar reasons, irony was prevalent in turn-of-the-century American naturalistic fiction.

Hassan further argues that postwar existential novelists have found two literary forms to be uniquely appropriate vehicles for the expression of their alienation from society:

> . . . the poetic and the picaresque novels, the introverted and the extraverted forms, share a common denial of reality as we see it with our everyday eyes, the former conveying its vision through a grotesque or victim hero whose alienation defines the shape of the novel, the latter projecting its vision through a roguish or rebellious hero whose free actions upon the world still imply a private standard of conduct. (104)

Frankie Machine in *The Man With the Golden Arm* is certainly a victim "whose alienation defines the shape of the novel," while Dove Linkhorn of *A Walk on the Wild Side* personifies the rogue hero who progresses, in episodic fashion, through a succession of increasingly outrageous experiences and adventures. Dove Linkhorn could, in fact, be used to illustrate Hassan's thesis that the outrage which modern American existentialistic fiction expresses is not quite the same thing that one encounters in comparable European novels.

Citing Emerson, Thoreau, Whitman, and Twain, Hassan argues that nineteenth-century American fiction was dominated by a unique kind of innocence. The idealistic foundation of our nation and its frontier legacy bequeathed to the nineteenth-century American writer an intense faith in individual freedom and human potentiality. (Hassan does cite Hawthorne, Melville, and Poe as illustrating a dark side to this peculiarly American innocence.) This innocent faith resulted in a strong emphasis throughout nineteenth-century America on quests for Edens and utopias. Huck Finn can still hope to retreat from a corrupt, slave-owning society to "the territory." Hassan argues that because of this legacy of optimism contemporary American writers have responded to the post–World War II diminution of the individual by technology, bureaucracy, and the loss of religious and political faiths in a more radical way than their contemporary counterparts in Europe. Instead of Sartre's literature of commitment, the contemporary American novelist retreats to irony and introspection: "Whatever else he may be, the new hero is not created like his classic predecessors, in a social image" (111). Moreover, long-standing views of the form and function of the novel have undergone a process of revision: "The decline in realistic techniques, the dearth of public themes, the aversion to ideology suggest a redefinition of the function of the novel which in the past has always tried to keep its vision centered on the highroads of life. The redefinition of function has now made some of our critical categories—symbolism and naturalism, tragedy and comedy—nearly obsolete" (103).

Algren's postwar novels perfectly illustrate Hassan's point about the elusive nature of such classic dichotomies as symbolism and naturalism and tragedy and comedy in contemporary fiction. Moreover, Frankie Machine of *The Man With the Golden Arm,* Dove Linkhorn of *A Walk on the Wild Side,* and Ruby Calhoun of *The Devil's Stocking* are, in different ways, antiheroes in conflict with society. Dove Linkhorn is actually a kind of absurd and bawdy Huck Finn seeking a territory where none exists.

Still, Hassan's comments about the new form and function of the novel provide a clue for his ignoring Algren in *Radical Innocence.* Throughout his work, Algren continued to use realistic techniques, even though in his mature fiction he merged them with surrealistic elements of narration. Again, the degree to which the horror dominates both an internal and an external landscape in Algren's mature fiction has not been sufficiently recognized. Still, Algren never wavered from his commitment to a fiction dominated by public themes, a literature of engagement. Moreover, in his early fiction, Algren's vision was definitely shaped by an ideology—like so much American literature of the 1930s and early 1940s, *Somebody in Boots* is written from an overtly Marxist perspective. Even when Algren's faith in Marxism declined, his commitment to the urban lumpenproletariat remained strong. Algren's people exist on the margins of society—not because they reject it, but because it has discarded them. Existence within the urban lower depths appears to offer a unique kind of freedom to a Dove Linkhorn, but even this ironic freedom ultimately proves to be illusionary, a waking nightmare.

4

"That Damned Feeling":
Somebody in Boots
and *Never Come Morning*

A Depression novel, *Somebody in Boots* focuses upon the uprooted American lumpenproletariat. Its dominant tone is one of outrage, and its primary goal is Marxist social reform. Episodic in structure, it follows the wanderings of its protagonist, Cass McKay, from Great Snake Mountain in southwest Texas to New Orleans, El Paso, and Chicago. Two extended jail sequences, one in El Paso and the other in Chicago, dominate the middle and concluding sectors of the novel. As Cox and Chatterton point out, *Somebody* represents a critical moment in the development of the American road story, which, until Jack Kerouac, was always associated with protest (72–73).

Part 1 of *Somebody* is entitled "The Native Son," and Algren's novel expresses views concerning the necessity of Marxist socioeconomic reform which are similar to the vision underlying Richard Wright's 1940 black protest novel, *Native Son*. Algren and Wright were, in fact, close friends (Wright wrote a preface for *Never Come Morning*). Like Wright, Algren believed that if reform did not come to America the exploited might easily be led toward fascism. *Somebody in Boots* contains a quotation from Marx expressing such a fear: "The 'dangerous class' the social scum (lumpenproletariat), that possibly rotting mass thrown off by the lowest layers of old society, may, here and there, be swept into the movement by a proletarian revolution; its conditions of life, however, prepare it more for the part of a bribed tool of reactionary intrigue" (189).

Wright outraged both the political Left and Right by describing Bigger Thomas's unthinking identification with fascist demonstrations in Europe. Further, both Algren's and Wright's focus on the potential of the exploited for reactionary intrigue is related to a not-yet-formulated existentialist vision. Neither writer was ever a fully trusted spokesman for the proletariat because each portrayed a level of despair in his characters beyond the reach of social reform or revolution. In Algren, this despair is particularly manifested in acts of nihilistic violence among the lumpenproletariat.

Still, for most of the novel, Cass McKay is representative of the characters who dominated American proletarian fiction in the 1930s. He is innocent and sensitive, qualities which cause him to be repeatedly shocked by acts of violence and injustice. He is innately romantic and responsive to what little beauty he encounters. Cox and Chatterton provide an excellent analysis of the way in which Algren, in the first section of the novel, contrasts images of beauty and brutality (especially decapitation) to emphasize the disparity between Cass's temperament and his environment (68–71).

Cass and his family belong to Algren's class of dispossessed and anachronistic pioneers: "Texan-American descendants of pioneer woodsmen—they too had no roots. They too were become half-accidental. Unclaimed now they lived, the years of conquest long past, no longer accessory to hill and plain, no longer possessing place in the world. They too were rotting" (8). Such "half-accidental" people lack the requisite will and vision to carve any more Chicagos out of the wilderness. Cass, however, retains sufficient romanticism to be attracted by the open road's promise of freedom and adventure. Although he hears graphic accounts of rewards and dangers on the road from hobos camped near Great Snake Mountain, he is driven from home by a violent physical assault by his paranoid father, Stub, on his physically deteriorating brother, Bryan. Algren's inexperience as a novelist is evident in his overwritten description of Cass's reaction to the attack:

> Cass's mind went black and blank; he never remembered leaving the house. . . . He was going somewhere now where men were less cruel. Some place where he would never see human blood helplessly spilling. He feared all blood; he dreaded men who spilled it. . . . All his manhood he would live with evil: with men who hated and mocked and fought, with strong men who were cruel to weak, with men who were weak but yet more cruel, and with men consumed with a wanton greed. . . . He was never to see a blow struck or a man

beaten, in all his young manhood, but he would be sickened almost to fainting. (36)

Such excessive editorializing runs throughout Algren's first novel; later he learned the use of ironic symbolism for implied authorial comment. At any rate, Cass is now established as the innocent, idealistic hero venturing forth into a brutal and corrupt capitalist world. There cannot, in fact, be a great deal of suspense left—the reader knows that Cass will undergo repeated victimization from cruel and greedy men without surrendering his inherent innocence and idealism. He is the pure knight of the lumpenproletariat, setting forth in quest of the grail of economic justice and freedom. Initially, there is even a pure maiden, Cass's sister Nancy, to complete the vision.

Cass's first journey lasts little more than a week. In New Orleans, he is knocked unconscious, mutilated with a knife, and left by a prostitute and her pimp to die in a garbage dump. He survives the experience but decides it is time to return to Great Snake Mountain. From the first, he has felt the residue of corruption and despair beneath New Orleans's façade of opportunity and freedom: "[Cass] saw black children who played within sight and smell of unmentionable filth, in alleys where gray rats ran. He saw the clean children of the rich, that they were quick and bold. On Melpomene Street he saw a young Negress with a baby on her back, pawing in a garbage barrel like an angular black cat" (50). The pervasive evil of capitalism has spread throughout urban America. Yet, when Cass returns home, he quickly discovers that things are even worse in Great Snake Mountain. Stub's paranoia has resulted in his murdering a man by pushing him beneath a speeding train; he is in danger of being lynched. A severe drought has descended on the region, and the men are anxious to kill. Thus, an innocent black man is "dragged through the streets behind an automobile, and burned" (67). Yet, for Cass, the one truly unbearable aspect of his homecoming is the corruption of Nancy, who has surrendered her purity to the harsh insistence of poverty.

Realizing that he must return to the dangers of the road, he first curses his sister: " 'Ah'll take out o' town direc'ly, an' then y'all go down valleyway like you said wunst, to get yo'self a job in a spik whorehouse in La Feria. . . .' It was his sister that was gone, not his father" (89). Purity has vanished from Cass's world, but he will continue to search for it in the most unlikely places. Cox and Chatterton see Cass's denunciation of Nancy as the first example of a recurring Algren motif—betrayal of love by a central male character which results in self-destructive guilt (68).

Cass's second experience on the road is even worse than his first. It is an unrelenting descent into horror and degradation—it would, in fact, be difficult to imagine any specific horror that Cass does not encounter. Algren utilizes Dreiserian documentation more extensively here than in his later books. As with Kuprin in *Yama,* Algren's purpose is to shock the reader into accepting reform. There are several descriptions of Cass and the other "road boys" pillaging garbage bins for food. The Christian, capitalist society attempts to deny them even this much: ". . . once a week, on Saturday, all open garbage was sprayed by the city. (In order to keep paupers from poisoning themselves on Sunday, which was the Sabbath.)" (126). Two brutal rapes are described: one a gang rape of a black woman by male vagrants, the other an attack by Cass on a child disguised as a road woman. Cass assaults the ten-year-old girl primarily because she initially reminds him of Nancy. Seeking the lost grail of innocence, he intensifies his guilt.

This experience does not cause him to abandon the search for a Nancy, and in Chicago he thinks he has found her in the person of Norah Egan. Like Cass, Norah is initially described in a manner appropriate to the traditions of the proletarian novel and American literary naturalism. She is first seen working in the ironically named Sunshine Frock Shop: ". . . it wasn't the slapping of a belt nor the incessant drone of many spindles, nor yet a low cloud of sweat-stench about her that Norah Egan minded most. What made things so hard, from the very first day, was not having water from morning till noon and then not from noon until the power was closed. That's what made things so hard. From her very first day" (191–92). Norah's experience in the Sunshine Frock Shop is reminiscent of the despair felt by Dreiser's Carrie Meeber while working in the wholesale shoe house in Chicago—poor ventilation, inadequate sanitation, and prolonged hours make her physically ill. Norah escapes such drudgery only to sink into a greater horror. After a brief stint as an exotic dancer, she becomes a "hay-bag," the lowest kind of prostitute: "Girls who picked up drunks were called hay-bags, and straight-hookers wouldn't even talk to them. Pimps called a woman a hay-bag when to call her a whore would have been flattery. Landladies would house a straight-hooker willingly, but would tell a girl to get out if they learned she was a hay-bag" (224).

In order to survive, Norah becomes brutal and ruthless, no longer a representative proletarian heroine. For Cass, however, she remains a substitute Nancy. The horror he has experienced on the road has so distorted his view that he is blind to her rapacity. The two form an alliance based on petty crime: they become a pathetic urban version of Bonnie and Clyde. In Algren's world, criminality, in itself, is not incompatible with innocence because the real crime is society's exploitation of the lower classes.

The Cass-Norah team is broken up when the two bungle a robbery and

Cass is captured and sent to the Cook County jail. During his ten-month incarceration, he subsists on dreams of a reunion with Norah. *His* innocence is still intact.

When Cass is released from jail, the 1933 Chicago World's Fair is in progress. Algren uses the disparity between the capitalist excess of the fair and the suffering of the Chicago lumpenproletariat as an occasion for Marxist editorializing:

> Just as in the final stages of syphilis a dying prostitute is given an urethral [*sic*] smear, so did a World's Fair now seek to conceal the decadence of a city sick to death. This city was trying with noise and flags to hide the corruption that private ownership had brought it. The *Tribute* [parody of the *Chicago Tribune*] was its smear. The *Tribute* gave glamour to its World's Fair reportage, but said nothing of homeless thousands living in shelter, not a word about women being forced into prostitution under its very nose. . . . The *Tribute* was the World's Fair pimp. Its concern was for the money-bags of Lake Shore Drive, of Winnetka and Wilmette; it had no concern for truth. . . . (275–76)

The horror is primarily exploitation of the lower classes; the solution Marxist reform. *Somebody in Boots* is a novel of social protest.

However, it is not a novel designed to please the Communist party. The book's most shocking brutality is committed by members of the lumpenproletariat against individuals from the same class. Algren's use of the quotation from Marx indicates that his primary intention, like Wright's in *Native Son*, was to depict such senseless violence as the result of economic desperation. But, also like Wright, he gives it a dimension outside economics, and, thus, beyond any conceivable reform. In contrasting ways, two characters, Stub McKay, Cass's father, and Nubby O'Neill, a fellow inmate of Cass's in the El Paso County jail, embody this most frightening dimension of violence. Early in the novel, Algren describes Stub's rage:

> Why Stub McKay turned out such a devil he himself hardly knew. . . . He knew a dim feeling as of daily loss and daily defeat; of having, somehow, been tricked. A feeling of having been cheated—of having been cheated—that was it. He knew that he had been cheated with every breath he had ever drawn; but he did not know why, or by whom.
>
> . . . .
>
> In time he gave his pain a secret name. To himself he named it: The Damned Feeling. (3)

The origin of Stub's "damned feeling" is his position as a frontiersman without a frontier. He senses that the historical process has been somehow perverted so that he exists only as a relic of an earlier, heroic age. His paranoia becomes truly dangerous when in the spring of 1927 he loses his job and begins to hear evil ancestral voices whispering in his head. Then his insane violence twice forces Cass to flee Great Snake Mountain. A believer in nothing but "fighting and hymning" (3–4), Stub is most enraged by the sheer fact of an existence without meaning. He believes correctly that he has been cheated by poverty and economic injustice; but, above all, it is a perverse twist of history which has tricked him.

Nubby O'Neill represents a level of viciousness even more dangerous than Stub's "damned feeling." He is, in fact, the embodiment of Marx's warning about the lumpenproletariat's potential for reactionary intrigue. Not at all insane, he hears no ancestral voices, but acts out of his own lust for power. Having been arrested for vagrancy and for associating with a black hobo, Cass encounters Nubby in the El Paso County jail. In this extended sequence, Algren gives his title a new level of symbolic meaning. Earlier, "somebody in boots" had consistently referred to the brutal authority of respectable society—the enforcers of middle- and upper-class law. While Stub McKay is the disinherited victim of the frontier legacy, Nubby, whose name is the result of having lost an arm, is a grotesque exploiter of that same legacy: "Although Nubby O'Neill was from South Chicago, yet his right forearm bore the legend, tattooed in hair above the stump: 'Texas Kid. His Best Arm.' His appearance was . . . that of a man who had seen too many Western movies in adolescence" (156). With the clear consent of the jail authorities, Nubby forces a brutal, perverted legal system on his fellow prisoners. Nubby's law rests on two assumptions: he receives tribute from the other prisoners and has the power to abuse and even torture them when he so desires. Nubby represents a corrupt authority within the lumpenproletariat; it is not at all difficult to envision him leading a brown-shirt movement. He would probably oppose any meaningful socioeconomic reform since it would threaten his power.

Perhaps the novel's most brutal scene depicts the savage beating of Rivera, a Mexican-American prisoner. Nubby rules that he and the other prisoners will flog the victim's exposed buttocks with their leather belts. The torture does not stop until Rivera has received more than a hundred lashes. Cass's innate sensitivity causes him to be beaten next—Stubby decides that he did not lash Rivera hard enough:

For a moment, as he bent over with his own buttocks exposed, Cass was secretly proud that he had not swung hard like the others. . . .

> In the minutes that followed pain taught Cass that he must never again treat a
> black man or a brown as he would a white. . . . (171)

In this scene, and indeed in the essential characterization of Nubby O'Neill, Algren is dramatizing the use of racism by American demagogues to divert and thus control the lower classes. Algren's two oppressive systems of authority coalesce in the El Paso County jail sequence. The jail officials refuse to give the prisoners adequate food and, as a result, "[Cass's stomach] felt as flat and as thin as though somebody had been stomping upon it. Somebody in boots as sharp as his father's had been; as pointed as Nubby's had become" (173). Upon release, Cass surrenders his will to Nubby until they are separated and Cass discovers Norah.

In much of the concluding Chicago sequence, Nubby functions as a kind of supernatural being—Cass feels and fears the presence of the figure in pointed boots. Nevertheless, Cass forms a brief alliance with Dill Doak, a black Communist who personifies proletarian unity and integrity. Doak attempts to convert him to communism, but Cass is puzzled and frightened by Party demonstrations. (Wright's Bigger Thomas also reacts to the Party with fear and suspicion.)

At any rate, Cass's choice of either committing himself to Doak and the unity of the proletariat or continuing his career of petty crime should be clear. If *Somebody in Boots* had been a formulaic protest novel, Algren's central character would follow Doak's lead and become a revolutionary leader. Algren isn't writing that kind of book, of course, and Cass is blinded to this critical choice by his continuing search for Norah, the imagined vessel of purity. Ultimately, the choice is taken out of his hands by the abrupt and violent reappearance of Nubby.

The spokesman for ugly, distorted, lower-class authority first assaults Cass physically and then lectures him: " '. . . Five times in two weeks now I seen ya walkin' with a nigger. . . . You fergit 'most everythin' a body tries to learn ya, don't ya?' " (310). Cass immediately declares his loyalty to Nubby and he "never walked with Dill Doak again" (313). Algren has thus shown the corruption of his innocence. When Cass does find Norah, she rejects his proposal of marriage, confessing that she has a venereal disease. The novel ends as Cass unconditionally surrenders his identity to Nubby: "Nubby spun his cigarette in an arc toward the gutter. Cass spun his cigarette in an arc toward the gutter" (322).

Algren intended *Somebody in Boots* as a protest novel which would shock a guilty, suffering nation into Marxist economic reform. With the characterizations of Stub McKay and Nubby O'Neill, he issued a prophecy of reactionary intrigue if such reform was not forthcoming. Yet, the worst horrors in Algren's first novel are Stub's damned feeling and Nubby's ruthless lust for power, both of which seem outside the reach of reform. Perhaps Algren believed that a Marxist society would end economic suffering and thus eliminate the appeal of a demagogue like Nubby. Even so, his vision of the terror occasioned by sheer recognition of the material and temporal nature of existence was already growing, and it kept him from writing a standard proletarian novel. Instead, he produced a work which, though flawed, retains its aesthetic integrity.

Somebody in Boots never quite transcends its origins as a 1930s Marxist protest novel. Like Edward Anderson's *Hungry Men* (1935) which in form and vision it resembles, the novel is more interesting and readable than most fiction of its type. Both Algren and Anderson depart from the standard formula of Marxist Depression fiction. Their mutual insight into the inherent brutality and corruption of much of the lumpenproletariat meant that, while they may have been "waiting for Lefty," they weren't at all certain that social revolution could save the lumpenproletariat. Like Anderson's Acel Stecker, Cass McKay does not make the "correct" formulaic choice at the conclusion of *Somebody in Boots.*

Algren's vision of the internal corruption of the lumpenproletariat is, in fact, reminiscent of Maxim Gorky's *The Lower Depths* (1902), a work for which he expressed admiration. *Somebody in Boots* is not as naive as most 1930s Marxist protest fiction. Still, had Algren not matured in vision and technique considerably beyond his first novel, his significance would primarily be that of an historical curiosity.

Seven years intervened between *Somebody in Boots* and Algren's next novel. Since by 1942 *Boots* was largely forgotten, *Never Come Morning* was received as if it were a first novel; and in setting and form, it is, in fact, quite different from the story of Cass McKay. The first of Algren's two ecological novels, it depicts life in a Chicago Polish ghetto. Since Algren departs from this setting only for a police station scene and a concluding boxing match, the novel's atmosphere is claustrophobic. In fact, were the narrative strategy of the novel different, Algren might have followed the lead of the turn-of-the-century naturalists in exploring an exotic internal colony.

The nature of Algren's social protest has also changed. One can compare the protest of *Never Come Morning* to the implied protest James Baldwin perfected a decade later in *Go Tell It on the Mountain.* Baldwin depicts white society only briefly, and the reader feels the socioeconomic oppression of his black characters primarily through this device of relative omission. The Grimes family is so thoroughly locked into its poverty that the white world might as well be a continent away. Similarly, in Algren's book, one senses the larger Chicago as a vague but overwhelming presence, waiting to reach out, if necessary, and crush his young Polish-American hoodlums.

George Bluestone provides an excellent analysis of a uniquely Algren novelistic structure which first appears in *Never Come Morning*. Bluestone argues that Algren utilizes a structural device of "frozen images in which development and consciousness seem to be arrested" (31). After an early climax in which Algren's main character, Bruno "Lefty" Bicek destroys his love for his girl, Steffi Rostenkowski, all that is left is a progression of "frozen" time before Lefty destroys himself. Bluestone asserts that this novel, like its successors, is based on the premise that "the impulse to destroy love" "is tantamount to death" (31). Indeed, there is a sense in which most Algren characters seek death. If one lacks the will to seek transcendence over nothingness and the creation of an integrated self, it is the only way out of the horror of material and temporal existence. Algren's male characters typically lack such will.

The subterranean spiritual and emotional life of *Never Come Morning* is symbolized by the preference of Lefty and his gang for an existence literally beneath the city. One of their favorite recreations is shooting rats beneath the El with "a stolen b-b gun": "Nothing like that could happen on a playground. The children of the poor preferred the crowded adventure of the alleyways to the policed safety of the playgrounds and settlements" (30). There are parallels between Algren's description of the children of the poor and Wright's treatment of the black ghetto in *Native Son*. Both writers depict street gangs inescapably trapped within a suffocating existence. The ultimate horror is that the trap seems normal to the gang members; they seem to have accepted, unquestionably, the idea that sunlight and fresh air are not meant for them.

Lefty Bicek, in fact, prefers the shadow world beneath the El:

> His preference for shadows remained. Sunlight and daytime were hostile things.
> Even by night he preferred the tunnel of the El to the narrow walk of the triangle. As a child he had learned that the safest place to play was beneath the El. For the streets belonged to streetcars and walks to people who lived in houses and not behind stores or above poolrooms. Nobody but pigeons owned the littered places under the steep Division Street steps. (29–30)

In part, then, Lefty is a victim of environmental conditioning, of naturalistic determinism. As Bluestone and Cox and Chatterton emphasize, however, he must also be seen as possessing free will. The line between environmental determinism and moral choice is, in fact, more difficult to draw in *Never Come Morning* than in any other Algren novel.

This difficulty arises because Lefty, like Bigger Thomas, is portrayed as a loner who exists outside the novel's conflicting value systems. *Never Come Morning* is, again in a manner comparable to Baldwin's *Go Tell It on the Mountain,* a generational novel. The first generation Polish immigrants, like Mama Bicek, still worship an American dream of Horatio Alger opportunity. Most are passively resigned to the impossibility of attaining such a dream, but they still believe in its potential. Similarly, Baldwin's first generation black northerners left the South in search of the same dream; in the present tense of *Go Tell It,* they have already confronted its unreality. The children of Algren's Polish immigrants, as Cox and Chatterton point out, enact a bitter perversion of their parents' faith: "To the young Poles of the Damen-and-Division Street neighborhoods, success awaits only their emergence into the bargaining power of hoodlumhood . . . they belong neither to the old land nor to the new; they occupy a shadowed borderland between . . ." (98). While Lefty has clearly attained "hoodlumhood," he cannot completely dismiss the values of the older generation. Thus, he is alienated from his mother and, secretly, from his gang as well. In the words of Cox and Chatterton, he is too "soft" and "sensitive" to make a "total commitment" to his "urban tribe" (99–100).

In part, Lefty's softness originates in his own lingering faith in the American dream; but, more fundamentally, it is the inevitable manifestation of a moral cowardice. Like more than one fictional protagonist of the lumpenproletariat, Lefty derives his version of success from popular culture, and, as is also typical of such characters, he focuses upon athletics. Lefty's dream does have its ugly side. Just as Algren had done in *Somebody in Boots,* he demonstrates that the aspirations of the lower classes are not free from racism. Lefty imagines, early in the novel, a newspaper headline announcing his triumph:

"POLISH WHITE HOPE WINS TITLE! LOUIS DECLINES RETURN BOUT!"
. . . .

Bruno exulted inwardly: he had just returned undefeated with a wad of twenty-dollar bills, had married that little Sylvia Sydney and had just told the Potomac Street Station Captain, Tenzcara, where he could get off. (24–25)

Lefty's dream has just enough basis in reality to keep it alive. He does, in fact, possess ability both as a boxer and a baseball player, and the Sylvia Sydney allusion illustrates a capacity for romance deep within him. Lefty's dream is also interesting as a reflection of Polish-American failure to assimilate into the cultural mainstream—his fantasies consistently emphasize personal and ethnic vindication. The real boxer, Stanley Ketchel, is one of Lefty's heroes; his fictional counterpart, Pultoric, is another. While in jail, Lefty imagines winning the heavyweight title in a bout against the Jewish Pinsky who had unjustly won it from Pultoric, and receiving a pre-fight visit from his cheated idol: "Pultoric had come to Bicek and shaken his hand, saying that it didn't matter to him who held [the title] . . . so long as it wasn't a Jew or a jig" (90–91). Algren is again dramatizing the lumpenproletariat's potential for demagogic exploitation in the name of reactionary intrigue.

Neither the attractive nor the ugly aspects of Lefty's dream can ever be realized, however; and the impossibility is due as much to Lefty's character as to his environment. Despite his boxing prowess, Algren's young hoodlum is cowardly in the most profound way. His fear is not physical; it is a moral cowardice originating in a fear of having to confront his own emptiness. Bluestone and other critics generally see Lefty as fearing death— instead, it is the possibility of life, or 'essence,' that dismays him. Algren effectively dramatizes Lefty's moral cowardice through his betrayal of Steffi Rostenkowski. Lefty's inability to adopt fully the values of his gang is illustrated by his love for Steffi. In the code that defines reality beneath the El, the female is merely a sex object, and love is equivalent to emotional weakness. Because he is soft, Lefty cannot deny his love for Steffi; but his internal terror and his desire to be one with the street gang make him unable to accept it. What he can do is destroy Steffi, who is as deeply committed to life as any Algren character. His betrayal begins with one of the most flat and unfeeling seductions in modern American literature:

> "I ain't got it in me to fight you off no more," he heard her confess at last.
> Later the fly without wings returned. He saw it against the screen and crushed it there with his palm.
> "You got blood out of him," Steffi said wistfully, as though thinking of something else. (28–29)

Lefty's outsider role is emphasized by the guilt he later feels: "She had put trust in him, who had no trust in himself" (35).

Like the fly without wings, Steffi is to suffer much worse from Lefty. In one of Algren's most shocking scenes, Lefty takes Steffi to a carnival and afterward convinces her to have sex with him in a shack beneath the El. When they are discovered by his gang, the Baldheads (formerly Warriors), Lefty stands back and lets the entire gang rape her. During the gang rape,

Lefty gets drunk, trying to convince himself that he bears no responsibility for what is happening; but Steffi's repeated cry—"Next!"—shatters his attempt at detachment. Abruptly, with no premeditation, he attacks and kills a Greek youth who has joined the group lined up for a turn with Steffi.

Steffi's gang rape and Lefty's unpremeditated killing of the Greek constitute, for Bluestone, the novel's early climax. His analysis of the rest of the novel as a sequence of frozen or arrested moments is accurate—this scene irreversibly determines the fates of Lefty and Steffi. Lefty's fatal attack on the Greek parallels Frankie Machine's murder of the dealer, Nifty Louie, in *The Man With the Golden Arm.* Both Lefty and Frankie lash out in desperation at personifications of their own weaknesses; both need to destroy some physical representation of their inner fear and guilt. Neither, of course, can find absolution in an act of unpremeditated violence. Lefty and Frankie sense that the worst horror is within. By adopting a narrative voice which affirms the humanness of his character, Algren can give Lefty a dimension of horror ultimately closed to McTeague and Hurstwood. Lefty's acquiescence in the gang rape of his girl and his murder of the Greek are not explained as resulting from the brute within or katastates in the blood. His animalistic behavior is a product of environmental conditioning and his own moral weakness. Algren does not view Lefty with Sartrian regard as an object—he is a self-aware subject. The sum of his brutal actions do not negate his humanness—he is often savage, but never an exotic.

Later Lefty sees a kind of justice in his being arrested for a shooting committed by one of the other gang members: "Only Steffi R. could free him" (96). Yet, until far too late, Lefty does not try to save Steffi after the gang rape. Instead, he passively witnesses her descent into horror.

Now viewed as a ruined woman, Steffi is taken to Mama Tomcek's brothel, where she becomes the special property of Bonifacy, the Barber. The Barber is the counterpart of both Stub McKay and Nubby O'Neill. Having established himself as a controlling power of the vice and petty crime of Polish Chicago, he represents a perversion of the American dream of success. His success does not ease his bitterness; instead, he is tormented by suspicion: "And still Bonifacy couldn't feel sure enough. He could never feel sure enough about anything. They were always trying to cheat him in this country" (10). The Barber's paranoia is actually an immigrant variation of Stub McKay's damned feeling; just as Stub was betrayed by history, the Barber is the victim of American hypocrisy. That he capitalizes on that hypocrisy to exploit his fellow immigrants does not ease his rage. Like Nubby O'Neill, he has equated survival with an ability to trick and control others of his social class—he is ripe for reactionary intrigue. That he can have Steffi sexually any time he wants isn't enough for Bonifacy. He wants her love as well, and, when he is forced to realize her lingering devotion to Lefty, he sets in motion the destruction of the young hoodlum.

Algren's account of Steffi's life at Mama Tomcek's is Algren's first extended treatment of prostitution, a subject he returned to in both *A Walk on the Wild Side* and *The Devil's Stocking*. In *Never Come Morning* he approaches prostitution with naturalistic seriousness and irony, in a manner reminiscent of Kuprin. Again the horror is that there is outwardly no horror; brothel life is dull and routine.

Mama Tomcek's experienced wisdom and passages of ironic lyricism communicate Algren's view of society's responsibility for the continued existence of prostitution. At one point, Mama T. lectures bitterly about the safety guaranteed to "the john":

"... all it ever turns out, for him, is somethin' to tell the boys in the back room about. But for her, it can turn out somethin' that she'll never tell anyone about, all her life; she'll just remember it: what the matron called her 'n how it felt to be fingered around like a dog that bit somebody 'n even if she stays out of that kind of trouble, she still got to have her blood test regular Saturday mornin', to make sure *he* don't get dosed Saturday night. Ever' thin's fixed for her to do the worryin'. That's the law of averages too, sort of.
So there's no such thing as morals. ..." (184–85)

Throughout his writing, Algren consistently emphasized his belief that respectable society needed and maintained vice, thus compromising its essential structure of morality.

More artistically satisfying than such editorializing are the lyrical passages in which "the hunted" prostitutes are described as being pursued by the police through a surreal world of grotesquely shifting colors. The Mama Tomcek segment of the novel is important for reasons other than social protest. In it, Algren completes his characterization of Steffi, a believer in life, or 'essence,' trapped in a profession which is perhaps the ultimate example of meaningless material 'existence.' More than Mama Tomcek's, Steffi's prison is her body, caught in the relentlessly temporal. Inexorably, she begins to share Bonifacy's damned feeling: "They were all trying to cheat her here" (188). An additional level of irony is implicit in the fact that Steffi is, of course, literally correct in this assumption: "The enormity of being accessible to any man in the whole endless city came to her like a familiar nightmare. It was true . . . it was to herself this had happened and to none other" (190).

The horror hardens Steffi, but it never destroys her need to escape and her desire for life. She considers suicide but is incapable of choosing death: ". . . it was life she desired. That that desire in her was too strong for the lifeless place she must live in, that what she told herself was a desire for death was actually a desire for life. And knowing this well in her heart, her only true plans were plans to regain her life" (213). One of the most vital of Algren's characters, Steffi is also one of his most obvious victims of determinism. It is not only her environment that entraps her; she is also victimized by the moral cowardice of Lefty and the viciousness of Barber Bonifacy.

Steffi's rejection of suicide illustrates Algren's emerging existential consciousness. In an essay titled "Absurd Freedom," Albert Camus discusses suicide as the inevitable, but ethically unacceptable, temptation of "absurd man":

> Suicide, like the leap [into religious faith], is acceptance at its extreme. Everything is over and man returns to his essential history. His future, his unique and dreadful future—he sees and rushes toward it. In its way, suicide settles the absurd. It engulfs the absurd in the same death. But I know that in order to keep alive, the absurd cannot be settled. It escapes suicide to the extent that it is simultaneously awareness and rejection of death. . . .
> . . . Everything that is indomitable and passionate in a human heart quickens . . . with its own life. It is essential to die unreconciled and not of one's own free will. Suicide is a repudiation. (40–41)

Throughout Algren, female characters are shown as more capable than male characters of a passionate indomitability, of confronting the essential challenge of existence through a full acceptance of life.

In a powerful scene, Steffi is shown attempting to pray at St. John Cantius Church and to humble herself into accepting her fate as a just punishment for her initial sexual surrender to Lefty. She does "forcibly make herself think: Mea culpa, mea maxima culpa," but is unable to feel true humility (227–28). God, in Algren's world, offers no salvation—in fact, in suppressing the poor, He is an ally of the establishment. Steffi senses this and rejects Camus's other form of extreme acceptance—the leap into faith. Instead, Steffi decides that she must trust in Lefty for escape from Mama Tomcek and the Barber. But her new hardness enables her to see Lefty more clearly than she has before: " 'He didn't mean it bad. He just don't have no guts' " (247). In the most fundamental of ways, he has no guts; still he represents her only hope.

In addition to the account of Steffi in the Barber's captivity, Bluestone's concept of frozen time in the novel can be seen in two extended sequences involving Lefty. His arrest for the shooting allows Algren to describe, in a serious, angry tone, scenes to which he will return in *The Man With the Golden Arm.* In the later novel, the anger will be alleviated by absurdist humor. The novel concludes with Lefty's plan to free Steffi and himself from the Barber through a prizefight. Both the jail and the prizefight sequences demonstrate that Lefty's cowardice is not physical. The arrest for the shooting is primarily an attempt by the police to obtain his confession for killing the Greek. He refuses to confess anything, except to himself alone in a cell, his guilt for betraying Steffi. He proudly withstands a brutal, scientific beating from the arresting officers without revealing which member of his gang did the shooting or confessing that he killed the Greek.

In *The Man With the Golden Arm,* in police officer Record Head Bednar, Algren develops one of his most complex characters. But the social protest of *Never Come Morning* does not permit any characterization of the police as complex beings. Thèy are treated as one-dimensional objects of satire, the hired enforcers of a corrupt society. Naturalistic irony dominates this segment of the novel: "This was One-Eye Tenczara, eleven years on the plain-clothes detail, three promotions and brother-in-law to an indicted alderman. Above his head a red and yellow wall motto bore a square-faced legend: I HAVE ONLY MYSELF TO BLAME FOR MY FALL" (81). In addition to Tenczara, there is Adamovitch, the personification of the assimilated Polish-American who hates the ethnic group from which he came:

> . . . he didn't like this kid [Lefty]. This was a low-class Polack. He himself was a high-class Polack because his name was Adamovitch and not Adamowski. This sort of kid kept spoiling things for the high-class Polacks by always showing off instead of being good citizens like the Irish. That was why the Irish ran the City Hall and the Police Department and the Board of Education and the Post Office while the Polacks lived off relief and got drunk and never got anywhere and had everybody down on them, even their own priests. (127–28)

Algren utilizes his familiar police lineup scene in *Never Come Morning,* a device central to *The Man With the Golden Arm* and the short story "The Captain Has Bad Dreams." The controlling protest in this section of *Never Come Morning* makes any absurdist comedy impossible; here Algren focuses as much upon the safe, bourgeois spectators at the lineup as upon the prisoners: "Perhaps they [the spectators] saw no shadows. Perhaps they saw no man" (145). Norman Mailer tells of attending an actual police lineup in Chicago with Algren at which he says, "I could have sworn the police and the talent on the line had read *The Man With the Golden Arm* for they caught the book perfectly, those cops and those crooks, they were imitating Algren" (467). Lineups, in fact, served Algren as metaphors for respectable society's depersonalization of the criminal Other. Lineups are specifically designed so that spectators can view suspects without reciprocity—they are based on a variation of Sartrian regard. In *The Man With the Golden Arm,* the humanity of a suspect does ultimately demand recognition from Record Head Bednar, and this recognition plunges him into a variation of existential anguish. After the beating and the lineup, Lefty is sentenced to the Juvenile House of Corrections for the shooting he did not commit. In describing the House of Corrections, Algren utilizes grotesque detail for shock effect in a manner reminiscent of *Somebody in Boots:* "The cells at the House of Correction had not been cleaned in many years. To the corners of the cots bedbugs clung, one upon the other, whole generations clinging to the backs of the preceding generations while the next generation was being born above them. In clusters. Like grape clusters" (153). The social protest and naturalistic horror of the extended arrest sequence prevents it from attaining the existential irony of "A Bottle of Milk for Mother," the superb short story on which it is based.

Throughout the arrest sequence, Algren stresses the code which prevents Lefty from identifying his companion, who did the actual shooting. His fidelity to the code of the streets is sharply contrasted to his earlier betrayal of Steffi: "He had been straight with the boys, he had been regular. And to be regular was all he had ever been schooled to accomplish. Beyond being regular there was nothing expected of a man. To give more wasn't regular. To give less wasn't straight" (133). Still, he is plagued by nightmares about Steffi. Even his fantasies about Sylvia Sydney bring no release because, in the House of Corrections, the vision of the actress always turns abruptly into Steffi as she is being raped. By repeatedly stressing the guilt Lefty feels, Algren undercuts the deterministic excuse he has provided for his character.

It is artistically valid, then, that Lefty make a belated attempt to rescue Steffi. He does so by signing for a boxing match without the Barber's permission; since the Barber does control all activities of the street gang, his permission is required. Lefty naively dreams, however, that he will win enough money in the fight to buy Steffi's way out of Mama Tomcek's. The fight sequence, in which Lefty battles a black boxer named Tucker, is perhaps the best scene of its kind in American literature. Algren understands

53

the science of boxing, as well as the ugly blood lust of fight fans. At one point, the crowd becomes especially frenzied when it looks as if Lefty is about to knock Tucker out:

> *"Do it do it do it do it!"*
> They'd stood up in the rows here before to see the slope-shouldered Pole come in for the kill; they had learned to like the way he had won before, dropping his man forward and stiff as a board as though—who could tell—he were out for keeps with an inquest and all. Hadn't Baer killed Frankie Campbell. . . . (267)

Algren is especially masterful at utilizing the fight scene for a quick synopsis of the key moments in Lefty's betrayal of Steffi: "Something began going around in the back of Bruno's brain: 'You got blood out of him, Bunny. It's awright, you got blood out of him.' He backpeddled, trying to remember better: why had she called 'Next! Next!' like that?" (270–71). This reprise foreshadows the fact that Lefty is doomed, even should he defeat Tucker; after he returns to his dressing room in victory, Tenczara appears to arrest him for the murder of the Greek. Lefty passively surrenders, accepting his inevitable death: "Knew I'd never get t' be twenty-one anyhow," he said (284).

This concluding line is perhaps the ultimate expression of "the damned feeling" in Algren. It is potentially easy and perhaps hypocritical for an academic critic to sit in judgment on Bruno "Lefty" Bicek for his moral cowardice: his subterranean life has limited his potential for developing an authentic 'Self.' Yet Algren utilizes Lefty's guilt as the principal means of isolating him from the other characters in the novel. Such intense guilt necessarily arises out of an awareness of choice. It should be said that Lefty's guilt results entirely from his abandonment of Steffi and not at all from killing the Greek. Thus, while Steffi and the other characters are deterministically victimized, Lefty initially has the potential to transcend his environment. For him, the horror is both external and internal; he knows, like Steffi, that he has "no guts."

A comparison of Lefty to Richard Wright's Bigger Thomas should clarify this point. Bigger kills accidentally, out of fear of and rage at white oppression. He instinctively strikes out at a symbol of society's power over him and later chooses to believe he killed on purpose. Moreover, he creates a new Self out of this belief. In contrast, Lefty kills out of frustration at his own weakness, his victim as much a helpless pawn of society as he is, and he derives nothing but guilt from his act.

Never Come Morning contains sufficient social protest to satisfy Geismar's definition of naturalism, and it utilizes sufficient environmental determinism to satisfy Rahv's main criteria. Yet, in this book Algren moves closer to an existential viewpoint. His vision and art become more complex and universal than in *Somebody in Boots*. *Never Come Morning* dramatizes the awesome odds confronting any illiterate product of the ghetto who dreams of creating a Self which transcends physical and temporal existence. Surely Sartre felt this aspect of the novel when he chose to translate it. In his next novel, Algren would go all out and create his richest work, an even more complex blending of naturalism and existentialism.

5

Flight from 'Self' and Society: *The Man With the Golden Arm*

*I*n *The Man With the Golden Arm* all the richness of Algren's craft and vision came together, and the result is a uniquely compelling work, winner of the first National Book Award for fiction. Though the critical reception was largely positive, some critics indicated vaguely uneasy feelings about the novel even while praising it. Norman Podhoretz used his hostile review of *A Walk on the Wild Side* as an occasion for stating his reservations about Algren's earlier novel: " 'The Man With the Golden Arm' was a book full of half-realized attitudes identifying themselves only in a distant whisper; it was a book that never quite discovered what it wanted to say, which may account for the uneasiness one felt in reading it" (126). In fact, Podhoretz "never quite discovered" what Algren was saying. Still, one understands why the novel seemed confusing, and even confused, to those critics who expected straight naturalistic protest from Algren. Some reviewers, for instance, were preoccupied solely with the novel's then-sensational treatment of drug addiction. *Golden Arm* was never intended primarily as an exposé of narcotics addiction; in fact, the emphasis on drugs did not enter the novel at all until the final draft. Algren has said that *The Man With the Golden Arm* began as a war novel: ". . . I was going to write a *war* novel. But it turned out to be this 'Golden Arm' thing. I mean, the war kind of slipped away, and those people with the hypos came along . . . and that was it" (Anderson and Southern 39–40). If the war slipped away, its legacy did not. The novel is dominated by the kind of existential revolt that Ihab Hassan sees as the prevalent mood of post–World War II American fiction. *The Man With the Golden Arm* can also be examined in the context of W. M. Frohock's *The Novel of Violence in America* (1957): Frohock sees such writers as Dos Passos, Wolfe, Farrell, Hemingway, and Faulkner as responding primarily to man's entrapment within time, the medium of materiality.

Not an exposé, not truly social protest, *The Man With the Golden Arm* is a relentless probing of existential dread among Chicago's Division Street lumpenproletariat. The novel does contain, of course, an important political dimension. The war is one of two compelling subtexts which add to its richness and complexity. Lefty Bicek's shadow world beneath the El could function as a metaphor for the second subtext of *The Man With the Golden Arm*. Like all of Algren's lumpenproletariat characters, Frankie Machine and his fellow residents of Division Street endure a submerged, claustrophobic existence. Representatives of the corrupt power structures of the city and the nation which ultimately control the fates of the urban proletariat are invisible in the novel because they are invisible to its characters.

Frankie Machine's sense of the socioeconomic power structure does not extend far beyond corrupt aldermen and cops. Existing in a world of petty vice, he is even removed from contact with and awareness of the truly powerful leaders of organized crime. Even Nifty Louie, at whom Frankie ultimately lashes out, is an insignificant pawn of the mob. While Algren had a sense of that obscene alliance between organized crime and American political leadership on every governmental level which Norman Mailer so frequently and effectively satirizes, he refrains from commenting about the alliance in his fiction because his characters are oblivious to it.

At the end of *The Octopus,* Frank Norris can enjoy drowning his symbol of capitalistic oppression, S. Behrman, in a shipload of wheat. Intellectually, Norris and the reader know that the death of Behrman is not going to change anything for the California ranchers victimized by the eastern railroad men and politicians. Still Behrman's drowning in the shipment of wheat, the natural force which he had attempted to control, allows Norris to reassure his readers that cosmic justice, while delayed, is not dead. In Algren's world, cosmic justice is a bad joke and the authorial luxury of killing an S. Behrman is not possible. Frankie Machine's killing of Nifty Louie is a case of one insignificant pawn striking out at an equally insignificant pawn. The murder is not even of particular interest to the police until Officer Record Head Bednar is pressured by invisible forces "upstairs" to solve it. This pressure, in turn, results from a demand by the hypocritical bourgeoisie that it be solved. Thus, traditional social protest is largely absent from the novel because the denizens of Division Street live such a subterranean existence that reform is meaningless to them. Socioeconomic outrage, on the other hand, underscores every aspect of the novel. Algren was very much aware that some people were reaping real profits from the petty crime and sinister drug-dealing around Division and that it was, finally, the hypocritical American middle class—which would be repulsed by any contact with Frankie, the Sparrow, and the other residents of the ghetto—that permitted them to continue.

A passage early in *The Man With the Golden Arm* describes the relationship between God and the ward super. "God loans the super cunning and the super forwards a percentage of the grift on Sunday mornings. The super puts in the fix for all right-thinking hustlers and the Lord, in turn, puts in the fix for the super. For the super's God's is a hustler's God; and as wise, in his way, as the God of the priests and the businessmen" (7). In the face of this alliance between the police bureaucracy and a most secular God, the beat cop and the hustler are equally vulnerable. Only right-thinking hustlers, those who contribute to the super and to God, survive. *The Man With the Golden Arm* is an example of engaged, but deeply pessimistic, literature which denies itself any real hope for social change.

Such critics as Podhoretz were especially confused by the tone of the novel. For the first time in his fiction, Algren utilized the grotesque comedy that sharply distinguishes him from more traditional naturalists. Here, as in *A Walk on the Wild Side* and *Who Lost an American?*, Algren is a true rarity—a writer strongly committed to a naturalistic vision who *intends* to be funny. One can laugh at Frank Norris, especially at the incredibly overwritten McTeague-Trina dental chair scene, for instance. Generally, though, one laughs at a failure of technique in Norris—his loaded diction is often inappropriate to what actually happens. With Algren, one laughs in appreciation of the triumph of technique. The peculiar comedy of *The Man With the Golden Arm* was unfamiliar and thus disconcerting to many readers and critics in 1949. It is a Céline-like comedy in which one laughs in recognition of the humanness of outwardly grotesque characters; it is a comedy that originates in Algren's harsh compassion.

On this level of the novel, Algren severely tested his readers. There is, for instance, the amazing love triangle between the sexually rapacious Violet Koszozka, Stash (her "Old Husband") and Sparrow Saltskin. Sparrow, the "unincapable" punk whose roof leaks on only one side, is attracted to Violet by the ease of having her. Violet is attracted by anyone younger than her Old Husband, whom she regularly locks in the broom closet for punishment. Old Husband wants three simple things: to lean out his window and check the temperature, to tear the days off the calendar, and to get a

good night's sleep. He, in fact, doesn't mind the broom closet since it provides a sanctuary of rest away from Violet. Violet's infidelity with Sparrow
reaches its ludicrous climax in "the Great Sandwich Battle," an extended
absurdist scene which ends with the perennially victimized Old Husband
being arrested for disorderly conduct and Sparrow, still chewing on a sausage sandwich, climbing into bed with Violet. Violet, looking at the sausage
string dangling from the punk's mouth, decides that "it was better than no
love at all" (140). The Great Sandwich Battle is the peak of Algren's grotesque comedy—for fifteen pages he portrays three absurd characters being
thoroughly repulsive and then, with the brief reference to Violet's need for
love, affirms their humanness.

Among the other grotesque characters in the novel are the landlord,
Schwabatski the Jailer, and his retarded twenty-one-year-old son, Poor
Peter, who plants paper daisies in the darkened stairwell; Umbrella Man,
who walks the streets with "a battered umbrella strapped to his back" (102);
and Meter Reader, the devoted coach of the hopeless sandlot baseball
team, "the Endless Belt and Leather Invincibles, an aggregation that hadn't
won a game since Meter Reader had taken it over" (102). All these characters congregate at the New Year's Eve "coming out" party for Old Husband
(because Old Husband had just come out of jail), which is assumed to be an
engagement party for Violet and Sparrow.

But it is Blind Pig who represents Algren's tour de force in human
crumminess and perversity. Blind Pig is so outraged by his lack of sight that
he determinedly looks, acts, and smells as horrible as possible. His last clear
vision was of a burlesque show, and he leers perpetually at a runway that
exists only in his mind. Everyone wants to hit Blind Pig, but no one dares.

Grotesque comedy is, however, only one aspect of the novel, and the
prevailing vision in *Golden Arm* is closer to Sartre than to Céline. Its world
is once again Chicago's Polish-American community; but, in contrast to
Never Come Morning, the focus is upon an *adult* subculture of gambling,
drugs, and lesser criminality. It is divided into two sections, titled "Ru-
mors of Evening" and "Act of Contrition." The former is introduced by
the Kuprin quotation: "Do you understand, gentlemen, that all the horror
is in just this—that there is no horror!" Yet, Algren is here not depicting
prostitution as Kuprin had been. The central horror of *The Man With the
Golden Arm* is the existential anguish and nausea of its main character,
Francis Majcinek, or Frankie Machine. In the "Key to Special Terminology" included at the end of *Being and Nothingness, nausea* is defined as

the "taste" of the facticity [which Sartre defined as "The For-Itself's necessary
connection with the In-Itself, hence with the world and its own past" (802)] and

contingency. "A dull and inescapable nausea perpetually reveals my body to my consciousness." On the ground of this fundamental nausea are produced all concrete, empirical nauseas (caused by spoiled meat, excrement, etc.). (804)

The most famous example of this condition in existentialistic literature is probably Roquentin's encounter with the chestnut tree in Sartre's *Nausea.* Throughout *The Man With the Golden Arm,* Frankie Machine tries to escape from the perpetual consciousness of the contingency of his being in drugs and literal or symbolic prisons. These attempted escapes ironically only serve to make him more conscious of his body's entrapment in the material.

Though a kind of authorial afterthought, Frankie Machine's drug addiction exemplifies the limited determinism which is central to contemporary or latter-day naturalism. Frankie's habit originated in the unbearable pain of a war wound. The dealer first met Private McGantic, his name for the "thirty-five-pound monkey" which he carries on his back, as "a face forged out of his own wound fever in a windy ward tent on the narrow Meuse." Both the dealer and McGantic "had served their country well" (56). Frankie Machine is, in fact, a kind of casualty—a veteran crippled by a habit which originated in service to his country. Private McGantic is then the product of the deadly environment of war and comes to control Frankie Machine. Yet McGantic does not explain the dealer as the concept of the brute within explains McTeague. After its origin in war, Frankie's habit becomes something he cannot shake in large part because he is afraid to confront his guilt and the responsibility of creating a Self. Such complexity of motivation is, of course, central to literary modernism and underscores Frankie Machine's humanness. A fictional card-dealing drug addict might well have emerged as a savage exotic. By emphasizing the internal dimension of Frankie Machine's addiction, Algren produces instead a character of full human complexity. The thirty-five-pound monkey is not a metaphor for turn-of-the-century naturalism's brute within.

The novel opens with Frankie Machine in prison with his devoted follower, Sparrow Saltskin. The star dealer of Zero Schwiefka's long-running poker game, Frankie is not unaccustomed to stints in jail. Indeed, as Maxwell Geismar has observed, Frankie, like other Algren characters, welcomes prison as an "iron sanctuary" that temporarily suspends his "fevered and distorted hopes" (187). Frankie's world outside is one of accelerating desperation. He is trapped in one of the most destructive marriages in American literature and tortured by his increasingly uncontrollable morphine addiction.

It is necessary to emphasize that Frankie Machine would be a victim if he had never taken morphine. Algren succeeds in giving the alter-ego of Private McGantic levels of symbolic meaning that Frankie is unwilling to confront. Most of all, McGantic represents the existential weakness of Frankie Machine, the all-encompassing guilt that renders him unable, even unwilling, to leave behind the destructive reality in which he exists, until he is finally forced into suicide, Camus's ultimate flight from absurd freedom. The origins of Frankie's guilt cannot be isolated in any single sin, either of omission or commission; instead, his guilt reflects an indifference, a fear of life, which lies at the core of his existence. The dealer lives a life of Sartrian bad faith. Algren effectively foreshadows Frankie's guilt in the opening jail sequence. To pass the time, Frankie watches a roach struggling to escape from a water bucket. He promises himself that he will save the roach when he is himself released. But, when that time comes, Frankie has forgotten his vow and the roach has drowned:

> It was too late all right. Too late for roaches or old Skid Row rumdums; it was even getting a little late for cripples and junkies and punks too long on the same old hustle. The water-soaked corpse was only half afloat, the head submerged and the rear end pointing to the ceiling like a sinking sub when the perpetual waters pull it downward and down forever. "I could have saved him," Frankie realized with a faint remorse. "It's all my fault again." (25)

Malcolm Cowley sees this incident as important primarily for the way in which it gives "the familiar animal symbolism" of naturalism new complexity and meaning (89–90). Naturalists have long been fond of using passive reptilian or insectlike creatures to signify the societal vulnerability of their characters (for example, Steinbeck's turtle in *The Grapes of Wrath*). Cowley is correct in perceiving that Algren's drowned roach conveys a similar idea, while possessing additional symbolic value. One remembers especially Sartre's device of utilizing insects, such as flies, to symbolize the perversity of material existence.

What is most revealing about the roach incident is Frankie Machine's assuming responsibility for it precisely in order to fail and thus add to his already crippling guilt. Such a pattern characterizes all of his important personal relationships in the novel. With each failure, Private McGantic grows stronger and more insistent. It is also important that Frankie's study of the roach begins as a means of passing time.

For Frankie and his wife, Sophie, time is the ultimate enemy. The medium of the physical and thus the origin of both life and death, time destroys their will as it heightens their dread of the sheer monotony of existence. From the first, their union is based on a hideously misshapen love that can be fed only by constantly accumulating guilt.

A careless reading of the novel might lead one to see Sophie as the origin of Frankie's problems. To insure herself against her lifelong dread of being left alone "with no one of her own near at all," she plays on his already unbearable guilt (33). Frankie has provided Sophie with a powerful weapon for binding him to her—in a flashback scene, Frankie takes Sophie drinking, gets drunk himself, and then, with his wife beside him, crashes the car. In the novel's present tense, Sophie thinks of this incident as "the blessed, cursed, wonderful-terrible God's own accident that had truly married them at last" (66).

The car-wreck scene stresses the novel's subtheme of wartime chaos and lost values. Frankie and Sophie have been drinking "A-Bomb Specials," a new invention of Owner's at Antek Witwicki's Tug & Maul bar. When Frankie passes out while driving, Sophie attempts to grab the wheel, screaming, " 'War's over, war's over, war's over for Frankie. . . .' " After the accident, a delighted crowd gathers: "All those for whom nothing had yet happened in the world shouting that it had happened at last." Frankie is shown sitting on a curb "with his army shoes in the gutter and his combat jacket ripped below the shoulder half-way to the overseas stripes below the elbow." Frankie wears the ripped combat jacket throughout the remainder of the novel; indeed, only death will end his war (67–71).

Physically, Sophie is not badly injured in the accident, but she suffers shock which leaves her crippled. Algren is especially masterful in delineating her trauma. A lesser writer would simply have made her a monster, stressing a conscious exploitation of the accident. In contrast, Sophie truly believes she is crippled, and Algren uses a mysteriously reappearing crutch with a cracked handle to symbolize her paranoia. In the novel's present tense, she keeps a scrapbook labeled *My Scrapbook of Fatal Accidence* [*sic*], filled with newspaper clippings of especially grotesque deaths (33).

In fact, her accelerating paranoia provides her with a horribly accurate perception of postwar reality. Chance, she sees, is the only god, and thus traditional morality is meaningless. Algren conveys her vision in a memorable passage of sustained ironic lyricism:

> For the city too was somehow crippled of late. The city too seemed a little insane. Crippled and caught and done for with everyone in it. . . . Nobody was at home to anyone else any more.
>
> . . . .

No one moved easily, freely and unafraid any longer, all hurried worriedly to work and anxiously by night returned. . . .
"God has forgotten us all," Sophie told herself quietly.
. . . .
The wind was blowing the flies away. God was forgetting his own. (96–99)

In a later passage, she states her vision much more succinctly and brutally: " 'It's just the way things would be if that Nifty Louie [the drug dealer] was God 'n Blind Pig was Jesus Christ' " (123).

Sophie envisions a far different world when she remembers her childhood and courtship by Frankie: "Years when everything was so well arranged. When people who did right were rewarded and those who did wrong were punished. When everyone, in the long run, got exactly what was coming to him, no more or no less. God weighed virtue and sin then to the fraction of the ounce, like Majurcek the Grocer weighing sugar" (62). (Sophie's nostalgic reminiscences of an ideal world exemplify Hassan's concept of the American writer's obsession with lost Edens.) Yet even then Frankie treated her with brutal indifference (62). Her war with Frankie began, in fact, long before the "fatal accidence." She has always struggled against his refusal to make a true commitment to her. In fact, Frankie is indifferent, not just toward Sophie, but toward everything except his drums.

Frankie's dream of playing drums in a jazz band symbolically functions in a manner comparable to Sartre's jazz recording in *Nausea*—it represents the 'authentic' 'Self' that he might create. Like Lefty Bicek, however, Frankie Machine has no guts and never intends to realize his dream. Instead, he tortures himself by fantasizing about the drums, and Sophie adds to the torture by ridiculing the dream. Both need these exercises in sadomasochism—Frankie wants any possible excuse for not attempting to realize his fantasy; Sophie senses that, should he ever confront the threat of 'nothingness' and risk the creation of an authentic being-for-Itself, he would no longer need her. Until circumstances literally force him to flee, she has nothing to fear. Frankie's indifference and resulting guilt bind them in a grotesque union.

When another fatal accident shatters the union, Sophie's paranoia is complete. She dreams of being crucified alone in her room by a mad Christ (300–301) and is last seen in a bare, white psychotic ward remembering "the sorrowful name of Frankie Machine" (311–13). Despite her manipulation of Frankie's guilt, Sophie is no monster; she is, instead, a victim of chance, environment, a too-rapidly-passing time, and her husband's unshakable indifference. Despite its prevailing seriousness, Algren's grotesque comedy does enter into the Frankie-Sophie relationship. Sophie begs Frankie to bring her a puppy; instead, he brings her Sparrow's Rumdum, an alcoholic "Polish airedale, sort of" and a denizen of the Tug & Maul.

Frankie also has important relationships with Sparrow and with Molly Novotny. Both are potentially healthier than the one with Sophie, though both are destroyed by a combination of circumstance and Frankie's moral cowardice. From the first, Frankie's friendship with Sparrow has its perverse side. The dealer manipulates the punk's mental incapacity with games that verge on cruelty. Still, as much as his indifference permits, Frankie cares about the punk, and Sparrow venerates the dealer: "If they'd been in the death house together he [Sparrow] wouldn't be too frightened so long as Frankie Machine was by" (6). The reader, too, responds to Sparrow. In the first half of the novel, the punk is involved in one ridiculous episode after another. Besides his affair with Violet, he attempts to strong-arm Gold's Department Store. The Gold's Department Store caper rivals the Great Sandwich Battle for comic outrageousness. Algren utilizes a particularly amusing narrative device in his characterization of Sparrow—he repeats the patently ridiculous alibis the punk gives for his petty crimes as if they were true. For instance, when Sparrow is caught having smashed a jewelry store window, Algren says that he "slipped on the ice." Sparrow's dognapping is referred to as "lost dog finding." This technique is tied to Algren's unique compassion for his characters; it is as if the novelist is saying that, if no one else will, he accepts the punk's face-saving alibis. Algren allows Sparrow the dignity of his creative truth.

Molly Novotny, or Molly-O, is, however, the most important person in Frankie's life. She personifies all that Sophie does not—passionate "indomitability" which demands life instead of death-in-life, love in place of guilt. She lives just below Frankie and Sophie in Jailer Schwabatski's and is initially involved with Drunkie John, one of Algren's Céline-like grotesques. Besides being an especially disgusting alcoholic, Drunkie John is sadistic. Molly-O stays with him essentially because she believes, in a different sense than Violet, that any love is preferable to no love at all. Molly-O wants more than sex; she desires love. Like Steffi R., she wants life above all; and, also like Steffi R., she dooms herself in her choice of a male companion, Frankie Machine.

Molly understands the destructive nature of the Frankie-Sophie relationship, knows that Frankie wants her as much as she needs him, and waits for him to free her from the world of Drunkie Johns. Her capacity for love is underscored early in some key dialogue between Owner Antek and Frankie:

ANTEK: "She got too bit a heart, that girl. . . . A guy can walk into her heart with army boots on."
FRANKIE: "There ain't many hearts like that no more, . . ." (30)

To an extent, Molly-O fulfills a function in the novel analogous to that of Nancy McKay in *Somebody in Boots;* she is a romantic ideal contrasting sharply with the intensely real and often sordid characterizations of Sophie and Violet. She also personifies that part of the dealer which yearns for psychological health and wholeness, while Sophie embodies his willingness to surrender to his addiction: "[Frankie] had found that, with Molly Novotny's arms around him, he could resist the sickness and the loneliness that drove him to the room above the Safari. . . . Only the blurred image of a woman in a wheelchair remained to darken his moods: that was the monkey's other paw" (113). Struggling to find the courage to face the "cure," Frankie realizes that "it would be Molly-O or a quarter-grain fix, he'd never make it alone" (120). It is Molly who gives Frankie a sharp "dressing down" and forces him to confront the psychological side of his addiction after Frankie protests that he has "lead in [his] gut" which " 'still hurts sometimes' ":

. . . "Don't give me that Purple Heart romance. . . . If things were right with you you wouldn't be runnin' to Louie because you got a pain in your belly. You're runnin' over there because you get to thinkin' the whole thing is your fault, that you smashed [Sophie] up on purpose. . . .
". . . you think your accident was made in heaven? Can that bull. It was made right down at the Tug & Maul at the bottom of a whiskey glass 'n you better start pickin' up the pieces 'n start livin' again with what's left over. . . ." (142–43)

Molly-O is, in fact, too much of an idealized, emblematic character, never as vivid as Steffi R. Algren's tendency to idealize selected women characters as embodiments of psychic health and momentary escape from sordid environments will possibly alienate feminist critics. While Molly-O does possess an undeniable human potential, her central importance to the novel's structure is as a projection of Frankie Machine's thwarted potential for salvation.

Ultimately Frankie's loyalty to Private McGantic proves stronger than any human relationship, and inevitably he goes to Nifty Louie for a fix: "[McGantic] was the fellow who looked somehow a little like everyone else in the world and was more real to a junkie than any real man could ever be. The projected image of one's own pain when that pain has become too great to be borne. . . . Frankie felt no pity for himself, yet felt compassion for this McGantic" (56). Louie is himself a reformed addict and, as he gives the fix, calmly explains to Frankie the source of the habit: " '. . . . When I hear a junkie tell me he wants to kick the habit but he just can't I know he lies even if *he* don't know he does. He *wants* to carry the monkey, he's punishin' hisself for somethin' 'n don't even know it . . .' " (60). In this particular case, Louie knows his man. Frankie's addiction is a manifestation of the guilt arising from his indifference.

Outraged by the fixer's power over him, Frankie lashes out and, without premeditation, kills Louie. The killing parallels Lefty Bicek's murder of the Greek in several ways. Like Bruno, Frankie acts without knowing he is going to act, striking in frustration at the personification of his own weakness. Moreover, the death of Nifty Louie destroys Frankie just as the Greek's murder destroys Lefty. As in *Never Come Morning,* this climactic moment occurs early; and, afterward, the novel depicts several extended sequences of Bluestone's frozen time.

Sparrow is the only witness to the fixer's death, and, almost immediately, Frankie suspects the punk of betraying him by stealing Louie's money after the killing. Ironic overtones to the dealer's distrust of Sparrow reverberate throughout the rest of the novel. The punk did not pillage Louie's body; he even provides Frankie the illusion of salvation when he talks the dealer into one of his inevitably bungled robberies. Frankie is arrested and once again welcomes the iron sanctuary of prison. This time, in fact, he vows to undergo the horror of the cure in order to come out of prison a new man worthy of Molly-O. He does successfully undergo the hell of withdrawal while in prison. Algren's depiction of Frankie's agony during the cure is intensified by his foreshadowing that it cannot last. Drug withdrawal does not, of course, resolve the dealer's guilt or remove his indifference. He is still a terrified man existing in a material, temporal world. As a fellow convict named Applejack tells him: " 'When guys like you 'n me get square we're dead' " (205).

Moreover, Frankie only agreed to participate in Sparrow's absurd robbery as a means " 'to kill the old monotony' " (180). That old monotony, of course, awaits him outside the iron bars of prison. Before his release, the dealer is fascinated by a distinct group of inmates: "They were the ones who had never learned to wait. For they were secretly afraid of being alive and the less they desired the closer they came to death" (208). Frankie's fascination with these men arises, of course, from his own secret identification with them. The old monotony awaits to remind him that he fears life as well as death—that, most of all, he dreads the challenge of creating a 'Self'.

Upon his release, Frankie returns to Sophie, vowing to start a new life with the drums. She, however, knows her husband: "But she'd seen spurts of golden hope in him before. It would wear off now as it always had. He'd be back dealing where he ought to be and she'd be sitting where she ought to be and everything would be just the way it had been, just as it ought always to be" (231). Molly-O has disappeared into the "neon wilderness" of the city, and Frankie is left with no one to reinforce his golden hope. Soon he is back in his card dealer's slot with "the old merry-go-round" rolling as hard as before (231). Quickly, it begins to roll harder as McGantic returns, as relentlessly insistent as before Frankie got square in prison.

Frankie's destruction of Nifty Louie has only made Division Street crime uglier and more brutally impersonal—Blind Pig is now the god dispensing morphine. Sophie's vision of Blind Pig as a perverted savior ruling a nightmare universe has come true. Sparrow, desperate and alone, his protector in jail, has become Blind Pig's assistant. When Frankie surrenders to McGantic's demands, Sparrow makes the delivery, and the resulting scene is one of the novel's most ironically powerful moments. Sparrow is now the master of their relationship, and he doesn't like the change. While administering the fix, he challenges Frankie, " 'It kills me in the heart, how you are now. . . . It just ain't like bein' Frankie no more.' " The dealer responds with a series of questions: " 'You know who I am? You know who you are? You know who *anybody* is any more?' " Sparrow, however, is not one for metaphysical speculation: " 'Be yourself, Frankie!' " (256–57). The punk, of course, has no way to know that he is demanding what Frankie is habitually too terrified to risk.

The scene ends in a police raid, and Sparrow, but not Frankie, is kept in jail. Frankie's release, however, is far from being an act of generosity. Officer Record Head Bednar, under pressure to prosecute someone for the murder of Nifty Louie, instinctively knows that Frankie Machine is the guilty one and that Sparrow can be trapped into so identifying the dealer. Bednar intends to keep the punk in jail until he does.

Frankie is now threatened by environment, as well as his own guilt-ridden indifference. Like *Never Come Morning* and indeed all of Algren, *The Man With the Golden Arm* utilizes a strong degree of naturalistic determinism. While Sophie's vision of Louie and Blind Pig as the gods of Division Street is its most powerful statement of environmental control, this theme is developed throughout the novel. In the novel's opening prison scene, Algren does explicitly tie Frankie's guilt to socioeconomic injustice:

> The great, secret and special American guilt of owning nothing, nothing at all, in the one land where ownership and virtue are one. Guilt that lay crouched behind every billboard which gave each man his commandments; for each man

here had failed the billboards all down the line. No Ford in this one's future nor ever any place all his own. Had failed before the radio commercials, by the streetcar plugs and by the standards of every self-respecting magazine. (17)

This extended analysis of the American guilt of the disinherited represents, however, the novel's only direct social protest. *The Man With the Golden Arm* is dominated by a social realism in which harsh, Céline-like compassion for even "the Republic's crummiest lushes" (16) has supplanted any hope for economic justice. Neither God nor the novelist "works any deep change on West Division Street" (7). Still, the novelist, if he is Nelson Algren, commits himself to a thorough, accepting portrait of the truth of West Division Street. The humanity of the Republic's crummiest lushes is undeniable.

So, at the end, Frankie attempts to escape both environment, symbolized by Bednar, and his own weakness, personified by Private McGantic. The reader knows that such flight is doomed—Frankie Machine's fate was sealed the moment he unintentionally killed Nifty Louie. Even in a world as completely fallen as West Division Street, one does not kill its god and survive for long. Bednar does trap Sparrow into identifying the dealer as Nifty Louie's killer, and extensive police pursuit of Frankie begins as his need for another morphine fix grows stronger.

Algren allows Frankie one illusion of hope before the end. He is reunited with Molly-O and reaffirms his love for her. This reunion is analogous to Lefty Bicek's belated attempt to rescue Steffi at the conclusion of *Never Come Morning*. In both novels, the central character attempts to embrace life long after the possibility of affirmation has passed them by. For a time, Molly succeeds in hiding the dealer; but, as the police close in, he can bear McGantic's torture no longer and hangs himself. (Shortly before his suicide, Frankie is wounded in the heel while fleeing from the police. The classical echoes of this injury illustrate the modernist complexity of the novel's rich symbolism.) In contrast to Steffi R., Frankie gives himself up to Camus's extreme acceptance of the absurd. Before dying alone in his room, Frankie privately says goodbye to Molly-O and Sophie, the two women who have embodied for him the challenge of life and the monotony of existence.

Referring specifically to Frankie Machine's flight from the police, Algren has said that he regrets *The Man With the Golden Arm*'s "cowboy-and-Indian ending" because it detracts from the novel's real tragedy, "the American disease of isolation." Had he written the novel again, he would have stressed more strongly "this fear of living which has always infected our national life" (Ray 32). One sees Algren's point; still, the ending of *The*

Man With the Golden Arm clarifies the complexity of his vision. As in *Never Come Morning,* environmental determinism unites with existential anguish to destroy a central character. The authorial emphasis in the two novels is different, however. More clearly than Lefty Bicek, Frankie Machine is a victim of his indifference, his fear of living.

Through the brilliant characterization of Officer Record Head Bednar, Algren gives his novel an additional level of complexity. For years during lineups, Bednar listens with weary contempt to the blatantly fake alibis of prisoners. Then, one day, he is told by a "defrocked" preacher arrested for writing a bad check that " 'we are all members of one another' " (198). The preacher's words stun Bednar; he begins to understand that his is the worst guilt of all. He has been a "traitor" in denying the humanity of those whom he has judged: "The captain realized vaguely that the thing he had held secretly in his heart for so long against them all was simply nothing more than a hostility toward men and women as men and women" (297). Bednar feels that "it was time to be stoned," but there is no place for him to go for redemption. So "Record Head wept" (298–99). In admitting his bond of humanity with the condemned, he admits his potential for committing any and all of their crimes. As Sparrow had tried to tell him, " 'Everybody's a habitual in his heart. I'm no worse 'n anyone else' " (276).

For years, Bednar has unconsciously protected himself against the pain of the suspects through a form of Sartrian bad faith. He has encased himself in his position of authority as a means of denying reciprocity with those in the lineup—he pulls out of the "file . . . in his head" (198) arrest slips which define the suspects as nothing more than manifestations of the Other. His identity has been that of police captain rather than human being. On this day, however, even before the defrocked preacher startles him with his assertion of a reciprocal humanity, Bednar starts to feel "the finger of guilt tap his forehead and the need of confession touch his heart like touching a stranger's heart. A voice like his own voice, confident and accusing: 'That's your man, Captain. That's your man.' A voice like his own voice. Yet a heart like a hustler's heart" (197). When the lineup ends, he abruptly perceives the suspects as innocents who disappear "through a green steel doorway into a deepening darkness" and the spectators as men and women artifically shielded from a recognition of the reciprocal humanity of those whom they come to witness and to mock. The spectators leave "through a well-lighted door into a clean, well-lighted street" (199). Bednar needs to confess that he has played the role of spectator-judge, witnessing and condemning the innocents. He has been a "grand inquisitor" defining, through the files in his head, those forced to appear before him as manifestations of the Other—he has been police captain judging the human

"Christs" of the ghetto. Now, too late, he wants to confess his humanness, his own capacity for "felonious acts"; but there is no one to hear his confession. Bednar's 'anguish' is his forced realization that nothing can guarantee the value of the inhuman values he has chosen.

The Man With the Golden Arm is an overwhelmingly secular work. God is worse than dead—he is Nifty Louie and Blind Pig. Still, through Bednar's epiphany of the brotherhood of the condemned, Algren introduces an element of Christian existentialism into the novel. All men are Christ; Christ is all men. Even on Division Street, mankind is sacred, the only source of salvation and forgiveness. More than once, Algren expressed his admiration for Dostoyevsky. In addition, the preacher's assertion that "we are all members of one another" recalls Whitman's faith in an American secular divinity, a uniquely individualistic affirmation of utopia.

The novel closes with an epitaph: a poem titled "The Man With the Golden Arm." It is a tribute to Frankie Machine's legendary skill as a dealer. Algren was fortunate in virtually every aspect of his third novel. Written and published before the novel, the poem nevertheless works as an ironic tribute to the dealer's immortality on Division Street. What the reader knows, of course, is that Frankie Machine's moral cowardice culminating in his suicide made his destruction inevitable. He never had the courage to attempt transcendence through the creation of an ethical center to his Being. He retreated always from the challenge of attaining essence. That he is remembered for his mechanical ability with a deck of cards rather than for any accomplishment with the drums is the final ironic statement concerning Frankie Machine. Indeed, his lack of an authentic 'Self' makes it appropriate that he is known, in life and in death, as the "machine."

The Man With the Golden Arm is a rich, complex work. Algren never wrote anything else quite like it. The richness of the novel can be illustrated through comparison to Willard Motley's 1947 novel, *Knock on Any Door*. Motley was a fellow Chicago novelist with whom Algren was and still is sometimes compared. A black writer, Motley avoided overtly black themes and depicted in *Knock on Any Door* the progressive destruction by society of a young Italian product of the slums, Nick "Pretty Boy" Romano. Initially a kind of innocent, Nick is brutalized throughout his life by the urban landscape in which he exists. Wrongly sentenced to reform school early in the novel, he experiences and witnesses unrelenting sadism at the hands of the school authorities. Thus, his fall begins. Released from prison, he encounters nothing but more physical abuse from his family and constant societal reminders of the boundaries which limit his freedom. Ultimately, he cold-bloodedly murders a policeman and, despite the eloquent plea of a liberal lawyer at his trial, is sentenced to death.

Algren knew Motley and personally liked him, but resented comparisons of his work to Motley's (Breit 87). Motley, he felt, only recorded the most glaring injustices of the city. Indeed, the criticism has validity. Read today, *Knock on Any Door* retains a kind of clumsy power derived from Motley's combination of naturalistic detail and moral outrage at urban dehumanization. It is, above all, a sincere first novel—the work of a writer emotionally committed to his subject matter and who has mastered, primarily through the influence of Richard Wright, the basic techniques of narration and plot. In fact, Robert A. Bone in *The Negro Novel in America* points out that *Knock on Any Door*'s plot is a near replica of Wright's *Native Son* (179).

Motley's novel is finally, though, a one-dimensional work. The author's honest (and legitimate) outrage at urban brutality leads him to create blatantly sadistic reform school authorities and policemen. *Knock on Any Door* contains several clear-cut villains for the reader to hate. Motley's outrage repeatedly pushes him to melodramatic excess. *Knock on Any Door* reads then like a sociological case study underscored by emotion and sentimentality. Nick Romano lacks any of the complexity of character of Wright's Bigger Thomas or Algren's Frankie Machine. He is totally and solely the product of a corrupt environment. One feels that all his problems could have been solved through meaningful social reform.

It is not this simple for Bigger Thomas who decides to accept the full meaning of his murder of Mary Dalton as the basis for a new Self or for Frankie Machine haunted by the guilt resulting from his lifetime of indifference. It is the internal dimension which Wright and Algren, in contrast to Motley, give to their characters which makes them memorable. *Native Son* and *The Man With the Golden Arm* offer no simple implicit solution to a horror which has internal, as well as external, dimensions.

As mentioned in a 1955 interview, Algren dismissed James T. Farrell as a "stenographic" writer who produces "social studies" (Anderson and Southern 46–47). While the validity of Algren's criticism of Farrell is debatable, his description of stenographic writers who produce straight sociological "case studies" certainly applies to Motley. A careful, dedicated stenographer can effectively document overt manifestations of urban violence and oppression. While such documentation has its value, it is an extremely limited form of art. A stenographer cannot reach internal dread and anguish. If Motley knew any Sartre, it was the Sartre of *What Is Literature?* (To a degree, *Knock on Any Door* illustrates the aesthetic limitations of an overly simplified literature of commitment.) Nelson Algren knew *Being and Nothingness* and *Nausea* as well. In fact, like Richard Wright, he knew the man, Jean-Paul Sartre, and his circle and discussed literary theory with Sartre and, of course, with Simone de Beauvoir.

Despite its emphasis upon drug addiction, petty crime, police corruption, and violence, *The Man With the Golden Arm* is ultimately not an exploration of an exotic urban colony. The unique triumph of the novel is that Algren, while portraying the world of Damen and Division in all its sordid crumminess, still communicates the complex humanity of his character. He does so by utilizing a narrative voice which reaches out to and identifies with his creations. As a result, the reader must grant them human reciprocity, no matter what absurd or grotesque acts they commit. *The Man With the Golden Arm* represents a crucial stage in the evolution of contemporary naturalism.

When he published his next "accidental" novel seven years later, Algren had largely moved away from a Sartrian focus on commitment to individual authenticity toward absurdist satire and a "harsh compassion" reminiscent of Céline. Although *A Walk on the Wild Side* lacks some of the thematic complexity of *The Man with the Golden Arm,* and despite its mixed critical reception, the later novel is in its own way an important, innovative work.

6

Experiments
in the Absurd:
A Walk on the
Wild Side and
Who Lost An American?

Algren outlined his concept of harsh compassion in a discussion of Tennessee Williams and Edward Albee. Speaking in the early 1960s, Algren stressed his preference for Albee's kind of art: "I prefer Albee's harshness. It's a harsh compassion with him. He's not as vulnerable. . . . He doesn't hold out any hope at all. Williams does, and I think it's not a true hope" (Donohue 231–33). Earlier, he had consistently praised Williams as representative of the "radical tradition" in American literature. It seems clear, however, that by the mid-1950s Algren's personal resentment and philosophical bitterness were pushing his own art in the direction of a hopeless surrealism. When he started revising *Somebody in Boots* for a proposed paperback reissue, he was "embarrassed": "I didn't want a book of such a title, and of such corniness, under my name" (Corrington 130).

In renouncing the corniness of his first novel, Algren was attempting to distance himself from *Somebody*'s overt Marxist protest and overtones of proletarian romance. Marxist reform was, he felt, as untrue as any other form of hope. Such negation necessitated an entirely new novel, one with a prevalent tone of satire.

As the critical attack on *Walk* accelerated, Algren's devotion to the novel intensified. Even though he might have gone all out only in *The Man With the Golden Arm, A Walk on the Wild Side* was his masterpiece—"the best I've written or will write" (Corrington 130). In part, such a conviction was defensive. Algren was hardly the first writer to defend passionately a work which had undergone severe critical attack; one remembers Hemingway's devotion to *Across the River and Into the Trees*. Still, Algren's judgment is much closer to being correct than Hemingway's. *A Walk on the Wild Side* is not only a good novel, but an important and influential one.

The book soon became a cult favorite. Ralph J. Gleason, for instance, has asserted that it inspired a new kind of American writing and that it has been echoed by such disparate figures as Joseph Heller, Ken Kesey, and Bob Dylan. Gleason sees the novel as a satiric inversion of the American dream set to a blues beat: "It's more than hard, it's impossible to trace some kinds of influences. Kesey's and Heller's debt to Algren is not only evident in what they wrote but in what they have said. Dylan may never have read *A Walk on the Wild Side*. Nevertheless he set it to music" (9). Algren would probably have accepted Gleason's evaluation. In a 1959 interview, he described his book in comparable terms: "It is a kind of novel that, so far as I know, has never been written before. It is an American fantasy, a poem written to an American beat as true as *Huckleberry Finn*" (Ray 32).

Certainly, *A Walk on the Wild Side*'s tone is a highly individualistic mingling of lyricism and satire. In fact, it is the tone of an American Céline, describing a long-vanished frontier. As mentioned, the novel's main character, Dove Linkhorn, is an ironic counterpart to Huck Finn. Yet, like everything else in the novel, Dove's characterization is largely illusion. While Huck Finn is a true innocent, an idealistic boy who chooses "to go to hell" rather than accept the corrupt values of adult society, Dove is a mock innocent, determined to attain material success even if such success means performing in live sex shows in a New Orleans brothel. Mark Twain described a rapidly receding pastoral ideal. Algren shows us an American nightmare in which the old pastoral ideals have become so inverted as to be almost unrecognizable. In his book, America has long since "gone to hell," and no program of reform can possibly retrieve it.

Algren wastes no time in establishing a pervasive satiric mode in the novel, which opens with a description of Dove's father, Fitz Linkhorn, a half-insane religious fanatic who entertains the bored citizens of tiny Arroyo, Texas, with sermons attacking their own sinfulness and the international conspiracy of "Papists Rapists" (*Walk* 10). The most faithful member of Fitz's "congregation" is his dying son, Byron, who continually interrupts his father's sermons to point out their embarrassing theological contradictions. The third member of the family is Fitz's illiterate youngest son, Dove. The Linkhorns are the McKays, now seen as absurd rather than tragic or dangerous. As Algren says, "Had there been an International Convention of White Trash . . . Fitz would have been chairman" (5).

Fitz is plagued by a variation of Stub McKay's "damned feeling": "The feeling of having been cheated. . . . Nobody knew why nor by whom" (*Walk* 3). Nobody knew except Algren, that is. Fitz's branch of the Linkhorn clan has always been cheated. Calhoun, Jackson, Jefferson Davis, and Lincoln ascended from corollary branches; but Fitz's immediate ancestors have continually moved west, "forever trying to keep from working with their hands," and have always arrived wherever they were going too late (5). This opening discussion of the Linkhorn legacy is, of course, a satiric variation of Algren's synchronic vision of American history. Thus, old Fitz has been cheated by a historical process and would, in fact, fail in any conceivable economic system. In large part because he is too lazy and incompetent, Fitz, unlike Stub McKay, will never physically threaten anyone but himself.

Algren's mock lyricism is especially effective in recounting the Linkhorn legacy:

> The road West now led only to a low, dark and battered chili parlor in what had once been the big, white and merry Hotel Davy Crockett.
>
> . . . .
>
> DANCING BY ELECTRIC LIGHT—that had pulled the bloods into the old Davy Crockett of Saturday nights. The wild boys . . . came to drink down their wild girls. Their girls that could drink down the moon. (19–20)

Linking the name of a frontier hero like Crockett to an urban black term such as *bloods* creates an intentionally jarring effect. And the wild boys cannot even drink down the wild girls. The old myths are ridiculed and turned upside down; and a bawdy surrealism results.

Significantly, there is no female counterpart to Nancy McKay in the Linkhorn family. In *Somebody in Boots,* Nancy embodied a proletarian purity for which Cass McKay never ceased searching. Dove Linkhorn is not about to go on such an idealistic quest. His ambitions are simultaneously less concrete and more worldly: " 'I don't know what kind of great I'm bound to be,' Dove considered his prospects calmly, 'all I know for certain is I'm a born world-shaker' " (56). Algren slowly unfolds the comedy of his character's sense of great destiny; Dove, in fact, doesn't discover what kind of great he is bound to be until he leaves Arroyo and arrives in New Orleans.

He does, however, become involved with a woman while still in Arroyo. Teresina Vidavarri is hardly a symbol of proletarian purity. What she does represent is quite complex and is central to a critical debate concerning the novel's ending. One thing about her is quite clear, however—Teresina is a classic victim. A woman of Hispanic heritage living in a drought-stricken region devoted to myths of male Anglo superiority, she is doomed from the start. A flashback describes her first experience with sex. At sixteen, she became engaged to "a bald, middle-aged Floridian of Spanish extraction," who turned out to be a pseudomilitaristic sadist. After that experience, she retreated to the wreck of the Hotel Crockett, vowing to forgo intimate relationships with men (23–25). Before falling victim to Dove Linkhorn, she kept her vow for ten years.

To Dove, Teresina represents the enticement of literacy and sex, both of which are related to the novel's subtheme of frustrated power. An ambition to read is the only residue of Cass McKay's romanticism to be found in Dove's characterization. Teresina owns a collection of fairy tales and reads to Dove from it. Algren thus introduces the ironic tale of a one-legged "steadfast tin soldier" in love with "a paper dancer dressed in lightest gauze" (31), which serves as an allegorical condensation of the entire novel. In true fairy tale tradition, the tin soldier is separated from the dancer and undergoes an extended period of pain and suffering before being miraculously reunited with his love. Of course, through all his ordeals his devotion never wavers. Three essential elements of such folk legends are thus emphasized: separation of the lovers, faith surviving physical suffering, and reunion.

Still, this is Nelson Algren's fairy tale; and, immediately after miraculously returning to the paper dancer, the steadfast tin soldier is "without reason or rhyme" pitched into a fire, "where he died" (31–33). The story upsets Dove, as well it should. There are parallels between the tin soldier's adventures and all that will befall Dove after he leaves Arroyo. More importantly, the tale's ending communicates Algren's new sense of determinism—man is the toy of external forces "without reason or rhyme" and thus beyond the reach of reform. He is the plaything of absurdity. Maxwell Geismar was correct in asserting that in *Walk on the Wild Side* Algren abandons almost completely the protest that dominates *Somebody in Boots*. His assertion that the late novel represented the "end of naturalism" is true, however, only if one accepts his equation of naturalism with protest. In an absurd world, man is entrapped by the most fundamental of external forces. He inhabits a material body doomed by time.

The tin soldier story symbolically foreshadows the demise of another myth. The American dream of equal opportunity has become only a grim joke in the twentieth century. Now, Horatio Alger would be, "without reason or rhyme," tossed into the fire. Dove, the "born world-shaker," avoids confronting this truth until the end of the novel.

Initially, he sees Teresina as the promise of literacy which, as every schoolboy knows, is essential to the Benjamin Franklin formula for material success. Idealistic values are, however, not all he sees in her. A growing and spectacularly healthy American boy, Dove wants Teresina sexually, and despite her vow to repudiate men, Teresina soon succumbs to Dove's advances. When she regrets her momentary weakness and refuses to sleep with him again, Dove brutally rapes her. While the rape is reminiscent of the recurrent Algren pattern of a central male character selfishly destroying love, it differs from Cass's denunciation of Nancy and Lefty Bicek's betrayal of Steffi R. in two significant ways. From the first, Dove simply lusts for Teresina more than he loves her. Most importantly, he is not, after the attack, tormented by guilt. Again, Dove's initial brutality toward Teresina complicates the implications of the novel's ending.

Like Cass McKay, Dove has listened to hobo tales of adventure on "the open road." Despite sensing "the uneasy guilt" "of homeless men" in such stories, he leaves Arroyo to fulfill his destiny of greatness (17–18). In contrast to those of Cass McKay, Dove's initial wanderings are largely comic. He instinctively perfects a mask of innocence which for quite a while protects him from serious harm. Besides *Huckleberry Finn,* Algren echoes *Candide* in his episodic account of Dove's adventures. Behind Dove's appearance of rural naiveté, there is, however, an inner core of cunning that, had he possessed it, would have saved Voltaire's hero considerable pain. Occasionally parodying Voltaire's language (Dove, at one point, reflects that "all was right with the world"[97]), Algren depicts a character who, for a while, beats the system.

For instance, Dove quickly learns to parrot an absurd formula for success which pleases exploiters of the road boys: " 'You got to work for nothing or you'll never get rich, that only stands to reason' " (99). It isn't difficult to see Algren's influence on Heller in such linguistic absurdity. Similar absurd inversions of the American success story establish the power of Milo Minderbinder in *Catch-22.*

In fact, Dove is true to the Linkhorn heritage and doesn't want to work at all, which is just as well since during the Depression there aren't any jobs. In New Orleans, he gets involved in two amusing con games. Both are based on experiences Algren had had and the first, an elaborate scheme involving coffee pots, results in one of the truly memorable sexual intercourse scenes in American literature. Dove attempts to retrieve a coffee pot from a young black woman more cunning than he is. As he attempts to grab "the genuine French Dripolator," the woman, sitting in a rocking chair, seduces him. The intercourse is accelerated when Dove is assaulted on the left buttock by a swamp mosquito. The incident causes Dove to experience one of his few moments of real doubt: " 'Sometimes I almost think it'd be money in my pocket if I'd never been born' " (131). The novel's bawdy sexuality, emphasized in the names of several main characters, is important for reasons other than comedy. Sex is the only true form of power which representatives of the lumpenproletariat such as Dove still possess. Even this power is, however, threatened by the prevailing horror, and Algren's treatment of it ranges from outrageous burlesque to brutal satire.

Dove's moment of self-doubt is short-lived because his true talents are soon discovered by a rapacious pimp named Oliver Finnerty. Truly one of Algren's most vicious characters, Finnerty is initially fooled by Dove's innocent façade. The pimp, having discovered the potential for profit in live sex shows, needs a male lead. Instinctively, he sizes up Dove as his future star and convinces the "country boy" to do him the favor of seducing a virgin. The "virgin" is, of course, one of Finnerty's girls, and without knowing it Dove is about to discover the "kind of greatness" for which he is destined. However "country" he may be, Dove Linkhorn is no Huck Finn, however. After accepting one hundred dollars from Finnerty for the virgin, he gives only ten to the prostitute. Later, he reflects upon his shrewdness: " 'It costs me ten dollars to make a hundred . . . at that rate I don't see how I can lose' " (164).

For quite a while, he doesn't lose. He becomes, in fact, the "Big Stingaree," deflowering Finnerty's "virgins" before appreciative audiences in Mama's brothel on Perdido (Lost) Street. Some critics, Podhoretz among them, view this segment of the novel as evidence of Algren's glorification of vice. But such an interpretation misses the point in more than one way. The novelist is anything but subtle in conveying Finnerty's brutality and cold sadism. He regularly beats the prostitutes and is masterful at exploiting their psychological vulnerability: "Finnerty's talent lay in his limitless contempt for all things female. He treated women as though they were mindless. And in time they began to act mindlessly" (198). Algren's characterization of the whores in *A Walk on the Wild Side* is reminiscent of Kuprin in *Yama*—both writers depict such women as exploited and brutalized victims. (Feminist critics will probably be no more pleased by this presentation of woman-as-victim than by such idealized Algren female characters as Nancy McKay and Molly Novotny.) Finnerty, in contrast, seems to have largely been inspired by Céline; he is one of a number of characters in Algren's novel who represent the human race at its crummiest level.

Dove's success as a brothel performer is, of course, central to Algren's parody of the American dream. He has capitalized on his one real talent and attained material success and even some local fame. In a world of inverted morality, it hardly matters how one rises to the top. Dove reflects, at one point, that all he wants to do is " 'make an honest dollar in a crooked sort of way' "(164). Such an ambition, according to Algren, is a small-scale version of how the American economic system *really* works. The only territory left for a Dove Linkhorn is Perdido Street, where Horatio Alger would be destroyed and Milo Minderbinder would prosper.

Dove prospers too, until he succumbs to an old ambition and a new emotion. The one prostitute at Mama Lucille's brothel who will not fall prey to Finnerty and who maintains as much pride as her circumstances allow is Hallie Breedlove (one of the more sexually explicit names in the novel). A mulatto, Hallie passed for white and taught school until the secret of her black blood was discovered. In disgrace, she fled to New Orleans and Perdido Street. Dove is instantly attracted to her intelligence and her beauty. Hallie, in fact, owns the identical fairy tale collection from which Teresina Vidavarri had read to him. Opening it, he again encounters the steadfast tin soldier.

Thus, Dove sees a new opportunity to attain literacy, the lack of which he believes is all that blocks his road to total success. Dove's obsession with literacy originates in his need for power. With Teresina, after all, he "only got to B" (166). Hallie, however, represents more to Dove than Teresina ever did, and the country boy falls in love with the mulatto prostitute. Ultimately, he persuades her to run away with him. The characterization of Hallie is in all ways more complex than that of Teresina. Despite her degraded position, she refuses to be a victim. With Hallie, Algren comes close to, but avoids, the male fantasy of the aloof whore—the seemingly vulnerable, but finally untouchable, female.

It should be said that Algren did attempt to avoid stereotyping the prostitutes in his fiction. For any Western male writer of the twentieth century, the challenge of providing depth to such characters is not an easy one. Because so many clichés and dehumanizing myths surround her, the prostitute emerges as an unreal figure—a being at once more and less human—in much twentieth-century literature. For a modern writer, making her believable requires a variation of the narrative principle of defamiliarisation or laying bare. The modern writer who attempts to humanize the prostitute must break through a substantial wall of middle-class reader preconceptions.

In his impressive recent study, *Difference and Pathology,* Sander L. Gilman thoroughly documents the way in which the prostitute, like the black woman, has been dehumanized in the West. The findings of late nineteenth-century "scientific" studies by Pauline Tarnowsky, Cesare Lombroso, and Guglielmo Ferrero have been incorporated into twentieth-century art and popular culture. Gilman cites Zola's *Nana* as an influential literary example of the depiction of the prostitute as a grotesque, subhu-

man being. (See especially his chapter titled "The Hottentrot and the Prostitute: Toward an Iconography of Female Sexuality.") As Sartre and
Simone de Beauvoir were well aware, depicting the Other as more than
human is simply another way to deny the Other's humanity. John Steinbeck's mindless whores-with-hearts-of-gold in *Sweet Thursday* and other
works exemplify this kind of condescending sentimentality. Podhoretz's
charge that Algren created similar characters says more about the critic's
lack of objectivity than the novelist's. Especially in the light of Gilman's
study, it is important to note that, even though she has black blood as well
as being a prostitute, Hallie does emerge as a complex, multidimensional
character.

Yet despite the complexity of Hallie's characterization, the long segment
devoted to her flight with Dove from Perdido Street seems out of place in
the novel. Its tone is quite serious, even idyllic, in places: "Here in the hour
of the firefly, while he and Hallie watched the lights of the Old Quarter
flicker, the happy time came at last to Dove. The one happy time. From an
unseen court or honkytonk, now far, now near, a piano invited them to join
the dancers. Each night they heard the same piano and knew the dancing
had begun once more" (270). Hallie does begin to educate Dove, moving
far beyond "B," all the way, in fact, to serious literature. Yet, with no warning, she leaves him; and his one happy time is shattered: "The last Dove saw
of the little room above Royal Street was a broken comb lying in a pool of
light. . . . In that hour when tugboats call and call, like lovers who have
lost their way" (284).

Because of the predominantly satiric tone and absurdist theme of *A
Walk on the Wild Side,* this sudden and intensely serious lyricism is jarring.
It is as if Algren introduces an element of courtly romance into a world
where such old-fashioned values are understood to be inverted and consequently comic. All that saves this segment of the novel is, in fact, Hallie's
reason for leaving Dove. Before meeting the country boy, she already had a
lover, Achilles "Legless" Schmidt, and she ultimately realizes that she can
never truly escape Schmidt's hold on her.

The legless man had an equally strong hold on Nelson Algren. More than
once, he described the Schmidt characterization as crucial to an understanding of all his work (see, for example, Cox and Chatterton 86–87). He
had previously created a prototype of the double amputee in his nightmarish short story, "The Face on the Barroom Floor." Legless Schmidt is
strong evidence of Céline's influence on Algren. In an interview with David
Ray, the novelist identifies a real individual, one Freddy from East St.
Louis, as the model for Schmidt: "I believe he was the strongest man I've
ever known. I don't mean just in physical terms. He had a strength of *per-*

son that dominated every scene he occupied" (33). Legless Schmidt also has a dominating strength of person in *Walk*. From the first, he affirms an individualistic code of acceptable conduct. Unable to get Hallie out of Mama Lucille's, he treats her with bitter contempt. The contempt is actually self-directed, but Schmidt maintains a façade of pride by constantly insulting the woman he loves and cannot save. He feels indignation at Finnerty's live sex shows and thus great contempt for Dove: "No, Schmidt didn't believe in this sort of thing at all." The double amputee has also constructed a wooden platform with wheels and has learned to maneuver it with great speed and dexterity. Consequently, he is disgusted by handicapped people who have not attained a similar independence. All in all, Schmidt is "a saint of the amputees" (253). Even more than Dove, Schmidt personifies sexual power. His double amputation illustrates society's threat to such power when it is manifested among the lumpenproletariat. Yet his characterization is dominated by the novel's most bitter satire. For instance, the name "Achilles" is an implicit and quite grim pun—the legless man has no heel. His genitals are, however, most definitely intact.

Schmidt's sainthood is Sartrian rather than Christian; he is closer to Genet than Christ. Originally he had been "ACHILLES THE BIRMINGHAM STRONG BOY," first a carnival performer and then a professional wrestler:

> Yet in the time it takes for a second-hand to move from twelve to six he had been beaten for keeps and his glowing manhood beginning so luckily, so clean, was smashed into something half-man and half-platform. Santa Fe freight wheels had proved even shrewder than he.
>
> What had been extricated, after hours of extremest pain in which he had not once permitted himself to faint, was no longer Achilles the Birmingham Strong Boy, but only Legless Schmidt. . . .
>
> If it had been his own doing, no one's fault but his own, it would be easier to accept even now. Yet, moving behind his memory there lurked forever the suspicion that he had been deliberately shoved over. At moments he could almost feel the hands at his shoulder, the knee in his back. (266–68)

Thus, he is equally driven by paranoia and pride. His paranoia is in part a perversion of his sexual pride. Whoever violates Schmidt's code of honor, consciously or not, becomes the target of his relentless hate.

Most of all, Legless Schmidt can be seen as Algren's personification of the lower classes. Mutilated by fate, driven by hatred and a stubborn residue of pride, he is beyond the reach of reform. Geismar's discomfort with *A Walk on the Wild Side* is easy to comprehend. Its central vision does indeed constitute a denial of the social protest so dominant in *Somebody in*

Boots. The prototype of the lumpenproletariat in the later novel is as insane and dangerous as the corrupt economic system itself; ultimately, his powerful sexuality will be of symbolic importance in his destruction.

Dove Linkhorn unknowingly arouses Schmidt's hatred simply by being who and what he is—a foolish braggart sexually exploited by Finnerty. When Dove runs away with Hallie, Schmidt's rage can no longer be controlled, and an apocalyptic climax is thus inevitable. When it comes, it rivals anything of Céline's as a picture of man's viciousness and "crumminess." Throughout Dove's idyllic interlude with Hallie, Finnerty has encouraged Schmidt's rage at the country boy. After all, the "easy mark" from Texas tricked the pimp out of ninety dollars. When Dove returns to Perdido Street after Hallie has deserted him, he abruptly finds himself trapped in a savage barroom brawl with Schmidt. As the assembled crowd yells its encouragement, Schmidt beats Dove's face into the floor (thus, the title of Algren's brutal short story, "The Face *on* the Barroom Floor"):

> And though, when Schmidt's fist was raised again everyone thought "relent"—panders and cripples and fallen girls, yet when it fell all felt a heartbroken joy. As though each fresh blow redeemed that blow that his life had been to him.
>
> Later, a woman who saw that the face on the floor was no longer a face but a mere paste of cartilage and blood through which a single sinister eye peered blindly, recalled: "When I seen him on the floor unable to rise and fight back, it went right through my mind—*Murdering. Murdering.* Why give *him* a chance?" (341–42)

Still, the nightmare is not quite over. The crowd savagely turns on the victor, wheels Schmidt into the street and shoves him down a steep hill where he smashes into a telephone pole and falls over dead, reduced to a lifeless "lump" (343). (Both the telephone pole and the "lump" are implicit phallic symbols.) The amputee does not resist his destruction: "And he took it, Schmidt took it, he took it all. Like a statue of grief with a sorrowing air, as though he had done nothing more than their own work for them: a saint of the amputees" (342). Schmidt's paranoia is vindicated; it is as if he has always known that his physical mutilation makes manifest the spiritual crippling of everyone around him. Thus, he accepts crucifixion at their hands. This climactic barroom scene anticipates Yossarian's pilgrimage through the streets and alleys of Rome in *Catch-22*—all the horror working behind the surface absurdity with only dark comedy finally exposed. For the Algren of *A Walk on the Wild Side,* the horror was an integral part of the nature of man, intensified, but not solely created, by socioeconomic injustice.

The climactic barroom scene is merely the novel's most memorable illustration of man's viciousness. Legless Schmidt is in fact redeemed by his proud code and his authentic, if helpless, love for Hallie. Certain other characters are hopelessly unredeemed. Besides Finnerty, there is Rhino Gross, "ex-physician, ex-abortionist, ex-quack, ex-man, ex-everything" and presently the inventor and sole retailer of "O'Daddy, the Condom of Tomorrow" (175). Gross offers Dove the following advice: " 'Look out for love, look out for trust, look out for *giving*. Look out for wine, look out for daisies and people who laugh readily. Be especially wary of friendship, son, it can only lead to trouble. And it isn't your enemies who'll get you deepest into the soup, it's your friends' " (181). Gross so despises humanity that his only real pleasure is leaving gaily wrapped packages of garbage on streetcars for strangers to find. Like Finnerty, Gross hates women most of all and is dehumanized by such irrational hatred.

Kitty Twist (another sexually explicit name), who appears randomly throughout the novel, should be conclusive proof that Algren's prostitutes do not have hearts of gold. Dove encounters Kitty when he first ventures on the road. They briefly travel together and Kitty begins Dove's initiation into horror. She describes her reform-school childhood: " 'Did you ever see four big men hold a girl down on a table while the fifth does the whipping? It was how they done me with a leather belt four feet long. It had a silver buckle I can't forget yet. And how they did drag it out! I could count up to ten between wallops. One hundred licks—I took the most they were allowed to give. And didn't cry Tear One. That showed I wasn't a crybaby' " (84). Not surprisingly, her experience has given Kitty a limitless capacity for savagery: " 'You know what the best kick of all is, Red? It's when you put a gun on grownups and watch them go all to pieces and blubber right before your eyes. That's the *best*' " (85).

Kitty drops out of the novel for over a hundred pages and then reappears as Mama Lucille's newest recruit. At one point she announces her refusal to be a victim despite her own contempt for her new profession: " '*Anyone* can be a whore. I feel rotten about everyone but myself' " (221). In the climactic barroom brawl, she is more active than anyone else in encouraging the savage violence: " 'I like to get up close to accidents' " (341). It is Kitty, in fact, who issues the initial command for the group assault on Schmidt. Kitty Twist's reform school experience gives her brutality a motivation lacking in the characterizations of Finnerty and Rhino Gross. Such motivation does not, however, make her the kind of sentimental innocent Podhoretz considered as representative of the Algren prostitute. It *is* an element of the old Algren social protest and, despite the novel's emphasis on the absurd, not the only one.

In *A Walk on the Wild Side,* in fact, one finds occasional echoes of the Marxist editorializing that mars *Somebody in Boots.* For various reasons, however, it is ultimately impossible to take such passages seriously. For instance, there is this satiric jab at President Hoover:

> "Nobody goes hungry," said Little Round Hoover, wiping chicken gravy off his little round chin. A man with the right stuff in him didn't need government help to find work. . . . Self-reliance for the penniless and government help to the rich, the Old Guard was in again. Hoover patted the chicken inside his pot. "I got it made," said Little Round Hoover. (97)

Satire of Hoover written in the mid-1950s inevitably seems more nostalgic than angry. More current and more serious are Algren's frequent attacks on the respectable middle-class "Do-Right Daddies" who frequent and then legally harass prostitutes. In these passages, Algren manipulates narrative voice to deny the reciprocity to middle-class readers. Yet, even they are usually distinguished by a tone of ironic lyricism:

> It was an ancestral treachery that do-righters practice. When opening time was closing time and everyone was there, down where you lay your money down, where it's everything but square, where hungry young hustlers hustle dissatisfied old cats and ancient glass-eyed satyrs make passes at bandrats; where it's leaping on the tables, where it's howling lowdown blues, when it's everything to gain and not a thing to lose—when it's all bought and paid for then there's always one thing sure: it's some do-right Daddy-O running the whole show. (108–09)

Algren's vision had evolved a great deal since the overt protest of *Somebody in Boots.* By the mid-1950s, he had come to see the evil as so ancestral and so deeply ingrained in the American economic system that all one could reasonably do was sing the blues. It was time to laugh at absurdity—certainly, art could not correct it. Anyone reading *Somebody in Boots* and *A Walk on the Wild Side* with no knowledge of their true relationship would be, at most, aware of some repetition of scenes and characters. He could not guess the second novel's accidental origin as a rewrite of the first. A blues song to the absurd, *Walk* contains just enough socioeconomic determinism to qualify as an idiosyncratic offshoot of naturalism. In its comic vision of horror and its manipulation of narrative technique, it is a truly revolutionary novel.

One last point concerning Algren's accidental novel needs clarification. Even Algren's most intelligent critics have seen the ending, in which a blind and disfigured Dove Linkhorn returns to Arroyo in search of Teresina as a kind of muted affirmation. Yet, given Dove's previous treatment of Teresina and the end of any opportunity to practice his one legitimate talent, it is difficult to see anything hopeful in Dove's return. What garden, one wonders, is left for him to cultivate? What Eden is left for him to find? He is blind and virtually helpless: the outlets of literacy and sexual power are largely closed to him. If there is any affirmation here, it is that unique acquiescence to pain which characterizes the blues. The blues are the lyric of the oppressed, and any vindication is thus Nelson Algren's and not Dove Linkhorn's. Dove has been to the "territory" and discovered a landscape of nightmare.

It is unfortunate that no matter how often he defended *A Walk on the Wild Side,* Algren could not quite believe that his work had been vindicated. He became convinced instead that his fiction was not wanted; and, until Rubin "Hurricane" Carter inspired another kind of accidental novel, he turned increasingly to nonfiction. He did begin a racetrack novel which he never finished, although portions of it are included in the 1973 miscellany, *The Last Carousel.* This miscellany also contains some daring material that Algren's publishers had deleted from *A Walk on the Wild Side.* But *Who Lost an American?* (1963) is the most interesting Algren work to appear after 1956.

Though *Who Lost an American?* has received virtually no critical attention and does not comfortably fit into any literary genre, it often has the creative power of Algren's best fiction. Dedicated to Simone de Beauvoir, the book is described on the title page in these terms: "*Being a Guide to the Seamier Sides of New York City Inner London Paris Dublin Barcelona Seville Almeria Istanbul Crete and* Chicago, Illinois." *Who Lost an American?* can be divided into four sections, each quite distinct in tone and authorial intent. The book opens with a short absurdist account of the mock innocent "Nelson Algren from Chicago" confronting the New York intellectual establishment. The broad irony here sometimes borders on burlesque. Next comes a considerably more serious account of the same persona visiting the capitals of the world. Especially in the Paris section, the tone is dominated by an elegiac lyricism. Abruptly, Algren shifts to comic nostalgia in describing his Chicago childhood and just as abruptly becomes savagely satiric in describing Chicago's, and America's, current corruption as "third-person" societies. The volume ends with an extended attack on Hugh Hefner and *Playboy* as the leading advocates of a "third-person" morality. Throughout, Algren includes extensive and often angry defenses of the aesthetic behind his fiction.

Any reader of Mike Royko will recognize the tone of the New York section. (Royko has often expressed admiration for Algren, for example in his recent book, *Sez Who? Sez Me.*) The Royko reader will be at home with the style and technique of the opening section of *Who Lost an American?* The "Nelson Algren" persona appears to be a midwestern rube awed by the sophistication of intellectual New York. Yet, through his gift for irony, Algren the writer communicates his vision of the sterile superficiality behind the eastern seaboard concept of culture. It should be emphasized that in this section of the volume one must distinguish between "Algren" as character and Algren as author, just as in such works as *Armies of the Night* one must separate the character "Norman Mailer" from his creator. This kind of self-characterization serves two main functions: it conveys a unique kind of narrative authority, and it places the work on a middle ground between fiction and nonfiction.

Ironically, Mailer is one of the main targets of satire in the New York section of *Who Lost an American?* He is referred to as "Norman Manlifellow, Boyish Author" (13). Algren especially attacks Mailer's much publicized pretensions as the principal heir to the Hemingway legacy in American literature:

> A fellow wearing a sandwich-board advertising himself approached me.
> "I am Norman Manlifellow," he introduced himself, sheathing a nine-inch jack knife, "Hemingway never wrote anything that would disturb an eight-year-old."
> He began working the lighting of the board by a battery concealed in his pocket, with the result that his candidacy for the Presidency of American letters was spelled out alternately in red and blue lights. (19)

It is, of course, easy to satirize the Mailer ego. What Algren always chose to ignore is that no one has satirized it more effectively than Mailer himself. Of course, Mailer's alternating praise and ridicule of Hemingway angered Algren, whose own loyalty to Papa remained constant.

Another target of Algren's ridicule is James Baldwin. Here again one suspects a personal motivation—Baldwin's own assault on a writer Algren admired. By the early 1960s, Baldwin had, in part as an act of self-liberation, written several essays attacking Richard Wright. For Algren, Wright would always be the main advocate for black consciousness. Thus, Algren ridicules Baldwin's assertion of universal white responsibility and guilt for black suffering.

Most of all the mock provincial (Algren) is, of course, satirizing the provincialism of New York City. He saw its fascination with the superficial as a real threat to the radical tradition of American literature. It is as if Algren foresaw the advent of *People* magazine and the current shallowness and cowardice of the American commercial publishing industry. He could not have been surprised at the triumph of how-to books and generic supermarket literature.

Still, it is unfortunate that Algren undercuts the validity of this satire by attacking Mailer and Baldwin. Behind the comic persona of "Algren" lies the bitterness of Algren, an unjustly neglected writer clearly jealous of successful rivals. James Jones is the victim of another unmistakably personal attack in *Who Lost an American?* Algren is much more successful and enjoyable when he kids Algren. Recalling his army experience in World War II, he writes: "I did not make PFC by happenstance. I just happened to be inducted when the army needed cowards in that classification" (12). Such passages remind one of Mike Royko's Slats Grobnik.

"Algren" soon finds himself at the mercy of Rapietta Greensponge of the prominent New York law firm, Doubledge, Deadsinch, and Pyrhana. The novelist had never forgiven Doubleday for its less-than-generous treatment of him during the publication of *The Man With the Golden Arm.* In fact, a jarring note in *Who Lost an American?,* as in *Conversations with Nelson Algren,* is the writer's bitterness over never having achieved financial security despite the commercial success of *The Man With the Golden Arm* and *A Walk on the Wild Side.* Such strictly personal bitterness does not, however, detract from the characterization of Rapietta Greensponge as an embodiment of corruption and cowardice in the New York intellectual establishment:

> Rapietta's face grew stern. "It means that our opponents have discovered that you marched in a demonstration protesting the bombing of Ethiopia in 1936, or somewhere along in there, and you have to get out of the country before you are subpoenaed. If this evidence comes to light they will be able to establish that if you had a mind you'd be dangerous! Our defense will go sky-high."
> "But I have never been at sea before," I protested.
> "You've been at sea for some time," Rapietta told me.
> I wondered what she meant by *that.* (10–11)

Rapietta's advice that "Algren" leave the country is the transition into the next section of the volume which recounts the writer's adventures abroad. It also foreshadows the quite serious satire of American imperialism which will be a dominant theme in this second section:

> "ALGREN": Did Ethiopia finally get free?"
> RAPIETTA: "They *must* have. They now belong to us." (14)

One wishes this first section were longer and that Algren had experimented with a comparable technique more often. In the remainder of the volume, the distance between Algren as writer and "Algren" as character virtually disappears. He utilizes an unmistakably midwestern burlesque only briefly, in the short section describing his Chicago boyhood. As this opening New York segment demonstrates, Algren was an extremely amusing man; but it seems that by 1963 his personal bitterness had become too strong for him to attempt sustained and potentially healing comedy for very long. Again, one regrets that his contempt for Norman Mailer was so strong that he could not see the liberating potential of Mailer's intentionally outrageous *Advertisements for Myself.*

In the overseas segment of *Who Lost an American?,* Algren the author and "Algren" the character are united. The tone largely alternates between nostalgic lyricism and angry protest at the human exploitation overtly and covertly sanctioned by American foreign policy. Wherever he visits, Algren seeks out writers who share his artistic commitment to the victimized. In Dublin, he meets Patrick Kavanagh: "He is the poet of the way it happened and the way it is; very close, in his celebration of man's ordinary hours, 'the arboreal street on the edge of town' or the bleakness of a hospital ward, to Walt Whitman. This is a poet to whom love is nowhere debarred" (50–51). He says of Brendan Behan: "The great Irish trick is to take care to hate most that which is farthest; so as not to be obliged to do anyone harm. . . . [Behan's] intellectual belief in the class struggle is modified by his emotional conviction that the only class is Mankind" (63). Inevitably, a visit to Ireland means recalling the Irish-American folklore of Chicago. In a few passages of such nostalgia, the comic tone of the first section is briefly revived: "Then there was Kenny Brenna . . . who used to sing *O Why Did I Pick a Lemon in the Garden of Love | Where Only Peaches Grow?* and Doyle the Irish Thrush!—a fantasist who billed himself as a heavyweight pugilist but was retired after knocking himself out on a ringpost at Madison Square Garden and yet he married well" (61–62).

In England, Algren discovers a middle-class hypocrisy regarding prostitution analogous to that in America. The women of Soho are supported, he argues, not by organized crime but by proper English husbands and fathers. Algren sees the same kind of hypocrisy as encouraging the existence of prostitution throughout all of Europe and North Africa.

In his descriptions of Paris, Algren's travelogue becomes elegiac. Such a tone is appropriate since the segment incorporates an additional element of travel, the journey backward in time to Algren's initial personal contact with the Sartre group of existentialists in 1949:

It was a time of beginnings.
All of my friends in that city were making beginnings.
My friends were Jean-Paul Sartre, Simone de Beauvoir, Jean Cau, Boris and
Michelle Vian, Juliette Greco, Mouloudji, and Olga and Jacques Bost.
Of these the most memorable face is that of Greco. . . .
She smiled. And the lights in the room came up a little.
That was Greco in 1949. (92)

Sadly, things changed in the early 1960s. Several key members of the circle
are dead, and Greco, having been discovered by Hollywood, now looks
desperate and haunted. "Castor [de Beauvoir] alone seemed to have gained
personal strength in the decade" (118).

The Paris section of *Who Lost an American?* is vital to an understanding
of Algren because in it he, for once, drops his pretense of knowing nothing
about existentialism. For instance, he praises Sartre's commitment as
preferable to Camus's isolation: Sartre, Algren argues, is "most dangerous
[to the establishment] because of his total commitment to the nature of man
and his opposition to formal assaults, from left or right, upon the nature of
man" (94–95). To Algren, commitment to the nature of man necessitated
acceptance of all that was absurd and even repulsive in human nature.

In a subsequent passage, Algren simultaneously pays tribute to de Beauvoir's brand of existentialism and foreshadows the last section of *Who Lost
an American?*

Existentialism, to her, was not a philosophical complex of Hegel, Kierkegaard,
Kafka, and Kant, but a means of living in the world with freedom and joy.

. . . .

[Existentialism] assumes that there is no alternative but to assume the responsibility of giving oneself: that the only way to be alive was to belong to the world
of men.

A decade later it appeared that the American *[Playboy]* key-holder and decided death preferable to risk.

. . . .

Existentialism directly opposed this view by going to its source, and to the
ancient biblical warning that to gain the world is to lose oneself, and to give
oneself to the world is to gain one's self.
This was the beginning my French friends were making in 1949. (99–101)

After reading his account of Paris, one can hardly take seriously
Algren's repeated pretense of philosophical ignorance. He had, in fact,
started to make the same beginning as his French friends before 1949. *The*

Man With the Golden Arm reveals how close his vision was to Sartre's and de Beauvoir's. In the early 1960s he saw America as morally seduced by the depersonalized, third-person values of Chicago's own Hugh Hefner. The horror then was the key-holder's victory over the committed man of ideas.

After Paris, Algren moves on to Barcelona where he is outraged by Spain's illegal and pervasive traffic in prostitution:

> When Franco has finished wiping out corruption in Spain he can come to work for us.
> . . . .
> Between Soho and the Rue Saint-Denis, Dublin to the Barrio-Chino, there is a vast wasteland that cannot be seen from any plane. A continent of young women abandoned more wantonly than sheep, than dogs, than cattle are ever abandoned. (131–32)

Algren believed that Franco's hypocritical war against corruption left the Spanish prostitute even more vulnerable than her counterparts throughout the rest of Europe. He believed, moreover, that if one understood American foreign policy he would know that the Spanish dictator already "worked for us" (131). The key-holder mentality had been exported throughout the world. Everywhere in Europe, Hefner's morality was in the ascendancy.

Algren is equally outraged at the power of the Spanish church: ". . . the Christ of Seville is a bejeweled colossus in the service of a medieval real-estate chain" (183). His visit to Spain, so very much Hemingway's adopted country, inevitably has its affirmative moments. While repulsed by bull-fighting, he is enraptured by Spanish dancing:

> Because whether the Spanish dancing is good dancing or bad dancing, it is always good dancing. For it says man is unconquerable.
> They tell me the Greeks gave us the concept of beauty and the Romans sound rules for keeping order.
> To me, the Spanish gift is the most precious. (188)

In addition, he visits the persecuted novelist Camilo Cela, who shares Algren's uncompromising commitment to humanity in all its manifestations:

> I asked Cela . . . what he would do if his worst political enemy were to be pursued by police and come to Cela's house for refuge. "I would hide him," Cela replied without hesitation.

This is, of course, the wrong answer for Rear-Echelon Liberals Against Fascism. . . . But it is the right answer for people who care about people. (155)

Ultimately, even Blind Pig and Rhino Gross cannot be denied forgiveness. Despite the beauty of Spanish dancing and the personal integrity of Kavanagh, Behan, Sartre, de Beauvoir, and Cela, Algren has discovered a world given over to "the American disease of isolation" and a resultant third-person morality. In an Istanbul café, he pretends to surrender to the inevitable: "[I] signed the tab 'Hugh Hefner.' In an absurd society all men are absurd except the absurd man" (206). The logic of the remainder of *Who Lost an American?* is aesthetically, if not philosophically, unassailable. Third-person morality has corrupted the world, and its leading prophet is one Hugh Hefner. Thus, the origins of the disease can best be studied in Hefner's, and Algren's, hometown: Chicago is at the heart of a sick universe.

Yet it wasn't always that way. Algren remembers a golden age of childhood innocence and purity. In describing his childhood, Algren combines the broad comedy of the opening New York segment with the lyrical nostalgia of the Paris section. He remembers his spectacularly unsuccessful father, whom he dismisses somewhat bitterly, but not without loving amusement: "How a man could work six years for the Yellow Cab Company and not get to be Foreman was what my mother failed to perceive" (*Who Lost an American?* 228). Whether a failure or not, his father had memories: "He had witnessed the fight between police and anarchists on the Black Road near the McCormick works. He had heard Samuel Fielden speak on the lakefront. Yet his most vivid memory was of Honeythroat Regan singing *If He Can Fight Like He Can Love / Goodbye Germany*" (*Who Lost an American?* 245–46).

Algren tells about the grief of his devoutly Catholic friend, Ethel, when her mother refused to pay the priest two hundred dollars to get her dead father out of purgatory. " 'He'll never see the face of Gawd,' " Ethel cried. Algren's father instantly had the answer: " 'Then let him look at His ass' " (234–35).

In contrast, the tone is intensely serious, echoing T. S. Eliot, when Algren describes the suicide of John the Greek, the ice cream store owner:

I began to skip cracks in the sidewalk. I skipped the crack with particular care when passing The Hanged Man's Place. Frost froze the cracks over and The Hanged Man's windows went white.

. . . .

Yet somewhere between St. Valentine's Day and The Place Where Ice Cream Came True I had realized that where God's colors raged behind a lifted cross was no business of mine. His colors were for people who lived upstairs. Not for people who lived down. (248–49)

The death by hanging of the secular Christ, John the Greek, began Algren's conversion to an existential god of the oppressed.

Yet, Chicago had remained, for a while longer, the true artistic conscience of the nation:

A search past country ball parks under a moon that said Repose. Repose. To where the 3:00 A.M. arc lamps of Chicago start, down streets that Sister Carrie knew. Everywhere men and women awake or sleeping, trapped with no repose.

The city of no repose that Dreiser found, that Richard Wright reached and Sandburg celebrated.

. . . .

A novel written . . . in the early 1940's, by the present writer [*Never Come Morning*] sustained the antilegalistic tradition which had distinguished Chicago writers since the early years of the century. (271–74)

In sharp contrast, the present Chicago culture is not only provincial, but resolutely ignorant:

Banana-Nose Bonura [first baseman Zeke Bonura of the old White Sox] once made three errors on a single play. Tony Weitzel of the *Chicago Daily News* once made six in a single sentence.

"Carlson McCullough," he wrote, "will appear here next week in his own play, 'Remember Our Wedding.' " After that it didn't much matter whether he got the name of the theater right or not. (281)

Algren would have been delighted to hear Chicago radio personality Wally Phillips, in the summer of 1984, plead with his audience for information concerning the identity of "somebody named Flannery O'Connor." (Phillips was apparently left in the dark.)

For Algren, nothing so dramatized the debasement of Chicago's proud cultural heritage as Hugh Hefner's enshrinement as the city's foremost authority on sex and everything related to it—thus, on everything. In *Who Lost an American?* Algren initially tries to joke about the Hefner phenomenon. He says that when invited to the Playboy mansion he discovered the legendary Chicago con man Terrible Tommy O'Connor, who had walked out of the Chicago jail in 1920 and disappeared, frolicking in the Grotto. " 'Didn't I tell you they built the system around me?' " Terrible Tommy asked (294–95).

Algren cannot maintain such a comic tone for long, however. To him, the *Playboy* phenomenon is deadly serious. Hefner and the famous "Playboy reader," actually hate and fear women and sex, Algren believes: "No matter that the maddened fathers of Salem dressed their women in black instead of bathing suits: the feeling toward women was the same . . . and as life that comes from women is evil, so women are evil. The force behind Hefner's image of a woman is one of contempt born of deepest fear. What he is selling is Cotton Mather Puritanism in a bunny outfit" (308). In truth, sex is an illusion in Hefner's universe. What is really revered is money and its power: "Hefner has perceived that the American businessman's most erotic zone is the skin of his wallet. . . . He'd run into trouble on his tax report if he tried deducting for a strip-tease act"—in contrast to a three-martini lunch served by a girl in a bunny costume (317). Fear and hatred of women, of life itself, equals fear and hatred of the Self and of humanity. No one wants to be involved in Hefner's world; all want instead the illusion of contact with an illusionary woman. Most of all, no one wants to be "I" or to acknowledge "us." The ideal is the Self as a disembodied "he" passing mechanically through a faceless crowd of "them." "The American disease of isolation" has reached its absurd climax. Third-person beings cannot communicate, and no writer can reach them.

It is not surprising that throughout *Who Lost an American?* Algren passionately defends his kind of literary commitment. If Chicago, America, and the world are as close to emotional, sexual, and spiritual death as he fears, a truly dedicated prophet is needed to counter Hefner and "the *Playboy* philosophy." The sense that it may already be too late does not deter Algren. "Such knowledge," after all, did not prevent Eliot, in *The Waste Land,* from preaching "the peace that passeth understanding."

Other writers whom Algren admired had demanded that unwelcome truth be heard. There were, for instance, Kuprin and Richard Wright:

Through Richard Wright we had become aware that those who ran the white world had lost the will to act honestly. We had learned from Wright that it is those who have nothing to lose by speaking out who become the ones to speak the truth. And to these, all the horrors of poverty—schizophrenia, homosexuality, drug addiction, prostitution, disease, and sudden death on the gambler's stairs—were no more remarkable than the sight of a man with a fresh haircut. In the midst of life, where there are nothing but horrors, there is no horror. (141)

Algren thus restates his view that the writer of integrity must perennially challenge the status quo: " '. . . any challenge to laws made by people on top, in the interest of people below,' I decided, 'is literature' " (152). The implied aesthetic here is clearly a limited one. On the most obvious level it implies a directly causal relationship between art and specific social and legal issues which one rarely encounters in lasting fiction, including Algren's. It is interesting, however, as an extreme statement of Algren's commitment to a narrative strategy of identification with the oppressed. Above all, Algren believed that the American radical tradition of literature must be preserved and defended.

Since only the artist can function as the conscience of society, the ultimate threat to art in a third-person society is assimilation of the artist into such a society. It is essential, then, that the honest writer follow the examples of Kavanagh and Cela. Algren vowed to do just that, in part because he saw too many American writers as having already surrendered to the disease of alienation. The tradition of Hemingway and Dreiser seemed on the verge of being irrevocably corrupted by the midde-class superficiality of Herman Wouk and Leon Uris. Such superficiality was, Algren felt, what the New York literary establishment desired.

Yet even the numerous passages pleading for a literature of commitment exhibit Algren's awareness of the complexity of the horror. It is too deep for traditional protest—third-person man, blind to everything, cannot be expected to see the most obvious victims of social oppression. Thus, the horror is largely internal—a disease of the mind and heart. Romantically, perhaps, Algren asserts his hope that the economically oppressed people of the world may yet be saved from third-person corruption: "Now in fishermen's ships moving at night across the Mediterranean, waking at daybreak in the huts of Africa or in the rooms below, millions unknowingly yet make the truths of our time. While wise men search the best hotels for news of Heaven. Never knowing that, every man being his own Barrio-Chino, true news of Man never comes but from below" (149). Now the writer must focus on, identify with, and speak for the lower classes, no longer in hope of improving their material condition, but simply to document their humanness. Perhaps the key-holder might still be capable of the shock of recognition.

Who Lost an American? is Algren's last major attempt to communicate and defend his credo. As the sixties progressed and the seventies arrived, he saw the world becoming more, not less, controlled by the absurd. The keyholder was, he felt, everywhere the arbiter of taste: Huge Hefner was selling advice about everything. The horror of Vietnam was followed by the cynicism of Watergate. Sadly, Algren never again attempted so radical an experiment in form as *Who Lost an American?* In fact, he renounced any ambition to "go all out" and attempt any more "big" books. Then, in the mid-seventies, he heard about the suspicious arrest and questionable murder conviction of a black boxer named Rubin "Hurricane" Carter. Even in a hopelessly absurd world, such a specific and blatant injustice, he decided, demanded investigation.

7

The Devil's Stocking:

An Experiment in "Faction"

Although the Rubin "Hurricane" Carter case now appears anything but clear-cut, and it may never be possible to establish conclusively Carter's guilt or innocence, this ambiguity does not detract from the aesthetic value of Algren's book on the subject, *The Devil's Stocking*. Published in the United States two years after its author's death, *The Devil's Stocking* is a variation on Truman Capote's and Norman Mailer's concept of nonfiction fiction or "faction." Capote, in *In Cold Blood*, is not ultimately concerned with the real Richard Hickock and Perry Smith. Mailer, in his recent "true life novel," *The Executioner's Song*, utilizes the actual condemned murderer, Gary Gilmore, as a representative of "the psychopath" as existential rebel and antihero, an idea central to Mailer's thought since his 1957 essay, "The White Negro." Thus, one's feelings about the real Gary Gilmore are not aesthetically relevant to *The Executioner's Song*. The historical question of Hurricane Carter's legal guilt is, if anything, even more irrelevant to *The Devil's Stocking*. However, the fact that on 19 February 1988 the attorney general of the state of New Jersey announced that he would not re-prosecute Carter is evidence that Algren's perception of the case may have been quite accurate.

While Algren closely follows the details of the murder for which Carter was convicted and the subsequent legal maneuvering, he gives his characters fictional names. Carter, for instance, evolves into Ruby Calhoun. The novelist, moreover, created one important character with no counterpart in the Carter case; Dovie-Jean Dawkins, a memorable Algren victim, unifies the novel's two main plots. It must be said that Algren retained his faith in Hurricane Carter's innocence. In an interview with W. J. Weatherby given on the day of Algren's death and published in his last novel, he discussed *The Devil's Stocking*: " 'In this new novel, I've tried to write about a man's struggle against injustice—that's the only story worth telling' " (12). Whatever its author's conscious intentions, *The Devil's Stocking* is about much more than one man's experience with injustice. Herbert Mitgang, in his foreword to the U.S. edition, places the book in the "muckraking" tradition (2). Certainly, protest constitutes one of its main elements.

Algren's commitment is, as always, to the oppressed. In the Dovie-Jean characterization, he again focuses on the horror of prostitution, while Ruby Calhoun is a victim of American racism and penal corruption. Although Algren dismissed James Baldwin's concept of universal white guilt, he expressed indignation, throughout his fiction, at this country's pervasive racial hatred, as, for example, in the El Paso County jail sequence in *Somebody in Boots*. He apparently believed that his investigation of the Carter case had given him the authority to write a novel primarily about black characters. Prison corruption and brutality, of course, are recurrent Algren themes. Cass McKay, Lefty Bicek, Frankie Machine, and Dove Linkhorn spend time in various kinds of penal institutions. Still, in *Stocking,* Algren gives the prison experience new dimensions of horror.

The novel's emphasis on racial hatred is intense and unrelenting. It is worth mentioning that Algren left Paterson, New Jersey, the scene of the Carter case, after repeated threats and harassments. In his final interview with W. J. Weatherby, he recalls his time in Paterson: "The hostility in Paterson was just about as sick as it could be. . . . Eventually it made me leave' " (9–10). In *The Devil's Stocking* he communicates what he had experienced. Racial hatred is a principal motivating factor throughout the novel and thus attains a power comparable to that of environmental determinism in traditional naturalistic fiction. In *What is Literature?* Sartre contends that traditional social protest remains a viable option for the black American writer, because racial prejudice is so pervasive and overt in America. In fact, Sartre's 1946 play, *The Respectful Prostitute,* is his own protest against American racism. Algren's book often recalls the best fiction of his friend Richard Wright. It is a tribute to Algren's genius that his novel does not seem simplistic in the 1980s. *The Devil's Stocking,* in fact, asserts that, despite the 1960s civil rights legislation, nothing fundamental had changed in American race relations.

A bloody race war, in which he is only peripherally involved, sets in motion Ruby Calhoun's ordeal. With one emphatic sentence, Algren establishes its background: "Nobody had foreseen the swift color switch, from white to black, which was consummated, within six months, that year in Jersey City" (28). He is describing an increasingly common demographic pattern in American cities—sudden increases in urban black population as white Americans abandon the city for the suburbs. Not uncommonly, the political and economic implications of such shifts produce potentially explosive atmospheres. One can cite, for example, the bitter anger produced by the election of Harold Washington as the first black mayor of Chicago, Algren's hometown. Paul Kleppner's 1985 *Chicago Divided: The Making of a Black Mayor,* is a revealing examination of the emotions triggered by Washington's campaign.

Since Algren is writing a novel, he must concretely dramatize the racial tension in Jersey City. Because of an apparently insignificant event—the purchase of a bar—five people die, two more are psychologically destroyed, and Ruby Calhoun is imprisoned for life. Matt Haloways, a "second father" to Calhoun, buys the Paradise bar from Vince LeForti, a psychotic white man who is very much aware of the color switch occurring in Jersey City. Because of his devotion to Matt Haloways's son, Red, Ruby regularly patronizes the Paradise. Irrationally devoted to Red Haloways, Dovie-Jean Dawkins feels that the bar is "home."

On the evening of 16 June 1966, LeForti, who has mob connections, enters the Paradise armed with a shotgun and demands money from Matt Haloways. Red Haloways, who tends bar for his father, has momentarily stepped out. Ruby Calhoun and Dovie-Jean are the only customers. In their presence, LeForti shoots Haloways twice when the black man does not immediately accede to his demands. The second shot is fatal. After his arrest, LeForti quickly confesses, stressing that he intended to kill Red Haloways:

> "I went down there and I took my shotgun. On yeah. Just one crack out of that redheaded nigger and he's going to get it. Oh yeah.
> "The redhead ain't there. So I shoot the old man instead. One is as good as another, they're all alike, makes no difference which one you shoot. You think I won't talk to a jury the way I talk to you now? The jury will love me. Oh yeah." (52)

While the jury does not "love" LeForti, it finds him not guilty by reason of insanity and commits him to a mental institution. On his release from the hospital, he discovers that he cannot escape the consequences of the murder. Jersey City's black population will not forget, and LeForti is constantly assaulted and beaten by black youths. Ultimately, he has himself recommitted. The LeForti characterization emphasizes the sheer insanity of racial hatred and the way in which it victimizes oppressors as well as those whom they oppress. Lieutenant DeVivani, a police officer, describes the psychological destruction of LeForti after his initial release: " 'Vince was always crocky, of course. Now he's really punchy. We can't let him carry a gun like we used to. He'd mow down anything he saw that was black, even if it were a cow' " (159).

Algren leaves subsequent events during the evening of 16 June and the early morning of 17 June 1966 veiled in mystery. The reader knows that after the murder of Matt Haloways in the Paradise, Ruby Calhoun and Dovie-Jean Dawkins attempt to enter the Melody Bar and Grill, an all-white establishment four blocks from the Paradise. After a brief, angry conversation with Dude Leonard, the Melody's bartender and a belligerent racist, they are refused service and leave. An hour and a half later, at about 1:30 A.M., someone enters the Melody armed with a revolver and begins firing. In a matter of minutes, Leonard and two customers are dead, and a third customer is critically wounded. Ruby Calhoun is immediately picked up for questioning and given a lie detector test. As part of an elaborate setup, Lieutenant DeVivani tells Calhoun that he has passed the test, when its results are actually inconclusive, and releases the boxer. Calhoun is later arrested and charged with the Melody Bar and Grill murders.

From the beginning, the state's case against Ruby is shaky; it is largely based on the testimony of two highly questionable witnesses, Nick Iello and Dexter Baxter, who are attempting a burglary near the Melody when the murders occur. Iello and Baxter, vulnerable to police pressure because of their criminal records and terrified of Calhoun's black loyalists inside and outside prison, repeatedly change and contradict their own testimony. The enraged white population of Jersey City demands a conviction, however; Calhoun, because of circumstantial evidence, his public visibility as a boxer, and his own record of petty crime, answers the demand. Without conclusively establishing Calhoun's innocence, the novel emphasizes the legal absurdities and the public hysteria that ensure his conviction. In this sense, Calhoun is clearly the victim of a racist society.

Calhoun's conviction also occasions Algren's extensive protest against prison brutality. In fact, prisoners in *The Devil's Stocking* correspond to the road boys of *Somebody in Boots*—they constitute a class banished by and from society. They represent Algren's last vision of an undeniably human, but universally despised, lumpenproletariat. Since *Boots,* Algren had learned a great deal about writing, and *The Devil's Stocking* largely avoids overt editorializing in its analysis of penal corruption. A highly intelligent character, Ruby Calhoun is always aware of what is being done to him, and he functions during his imprisonment as a convincing spokesman for Algren's point of view. Calhoun frequently discusses the penal psychology of dehumanization with Barney Kerrigan, a liberal public defender. At one point, he succinctly defines the conflicting functions of prisons and prisoners: " 'Prisons have only one function: to break the prisoner's ego. His own true function must be to hold onto it. Even though he is doing thirty-to-life, he *has* to hold on' " (145). The prison super confirms and elaborates on Calhoun's analysis. He tells Kerrigan that his prison is concerned with security and not rehabilitation: "Security is what the people of this state, who pay me, want. I cannot go against the voice of the people" (147). The super's assessment of what the people want is correct, according to Algren. The prisoners of *The Devil's Stocking,* like the lumpenproletariat of *Somebody in Boots,* have been condemned to a living death by mainstream American society. Their humanity has been denied; when the outside world thinks of them at all, it views them as animals who must be caged.

The super understands the necessity of destroying the prisoners' egos and has definite ideas about how this goal should be accomplished: " 'There is a right length of time for each prisoner—but you must never let him know how long he has to serve. What is most essential to security is uncertainty. When he goes into isolation you don't let him know how long he's going to be in there' " (148). If a prisoner complains too often, he is dispatched to the wing for the insane: "Once in the Bug Ward, the Bug Ward is your home. For keeps. If you're not a real bug when you enter, you soon will be" (149). Ruby Calhoun has read enough, especially books by Dostoyevsky, to see through and thus be immune from the super's psychological warfare.

The two central targets of Algren's protest—racism and prison brutality—come together in his account of a riot in the super's prison. Nightmarish from the start, the riot ends in senseless slaughter. Almost accidentally, the prisoners take a few guards as hostages and abruptly find themselves in a position of power. Given the systematic destruction of their egos, it is not surprising that they do not know how to utilize this new power. The riot soon disintegrates into a totally chaotic situation with different temporary leaders pressing conflicting demands on the penal authorities. Yet, largely because of the Black Muslims, no guards are harmed by the prisoners. The slaughter begins when an army of National Guardsmen and prison guards abruptly and randomly opens fire. Thirty-eight men, prisoners and guards, are shot down. Later, society's victorious army continues the brutality: "Nothing was reported about the beatings, administered by groups of correction officers, five or six in a group, upon blacks and Puerto Ricans held naked in their cells." Although he calls his prison "Athens," Algren leaves little doubt that the riot is based upon the 1971 Attica, New York, uprising, referring obliquely to Governor Rockefeller's mishandling of that tragedy: "No reference was made to Governor Nelson's demonstration of physical and moral cowardice" (212).

The riot occasions Algren's only lapse into overt editorializing, a long passage in which he further emphasizes his commitment to the oppressed:

> For the most heinous crime, that of demanding that men be broken to dogs, committed by society against the criminal, no mention was made [in subsequent press coverage].
>
> . . . .
>
> The confrontation was the state's. Because men are everywhere going to resist at being treated as less than men.
> The uprising had not been a race riot until the corrections officers made it into one. (210)

As in all his novels, Algren's loyalty is with the victims of social and legal injustice. Once again, the real evil is committed by society against power-less individuals.

But *The Devil's Stocking* is not only a social protest novel. Like Mailer's *Executioner's Song,* the novel has an underlying philosophy of Sartrian existentialism. Three characters dominate Algren's book, and only one of them, Dovie-Jean Dawkins, is a pure victim of external forces. Although a proud, independent figure, Ruby Calhoun suffers from a variation of "the damned feeling" which destroys Lefty Bicek. With Red Haloways, Algren shows a character resisting, even more desperately than Frankie Machine, the challenge to confront the 'contingency' of 'existence' and create an 'authentic' 'Self'.

Calhoun manifests an arrogant aloofness that makes loyalty to him diffi-cult, if not impossible. In the novel's opening paragraphs, Algren em-phasizes his character's self-destructive remoteness: "He liked people well enough and he enjoyed being liked by them. Later it began to appear that he enjoyed being hated by them even more. He built up friendships, it be-gan to look, in order to shatter them" (15–16). Inevitably, environment plays a part in Calhoun's antisocial behavior—at the age of fourteen, when assaulted by a white homosexual, he stabs the man with a scout knife and is sentenced to reform school on a charge of "atrocious assault." He feels no remorse about the incident: " 'I don't enjoy hurting people unless they mess with me. Then I enjoy it. If you mess with me I'm going to try to kill you. I don't fight by rules. I go for all. And I don't shake hands when it's done' "

(17). Before the atrocious assault, Ruby has been in trouble with the police because of his membership in a street gang, "The Elegant Gents," led by his friend Red Haloways.

In fact, Calhoun's youth is a continuous war against authority. It is not until he joins the army that he discovers a positive identity. From a Sudanese soldier in Germany, he first hears about the religion of Islam: "[The Sudanese] imbued Calhoun with pride in being black as Christianity had made him ashamed of his color. Islam awakened a moral sense in Calhoun" (18). Of equal importance, he learns to box in the army. Despite his new moral sense, Ruby's self-destructive arrogance dominates his behavior in the ring. He is hated because of "his curious habit of informing an opponent that he was chopping him up while chopping him up." He refuses to modify this practice: " 'Why shouldn't I be a fightie-talkie? . . . it's my business, my job. Would you tell a butcher to keep his mouth shut when he's slicing pork chops? It relaxes me' " (32). In America, it infuriates white spectators.

Calhoun is consistently loyal to principles, but never to people. Despite his faith in Islam, he remains separate from the Black Muslims while in prison. He makes no real attempt to hide sexual infidelity from his wife. Early in the novel, he seduces Dovie-Jean Dawkins, even though he thinks of her as Red Haloways's girl. Still, his destruction occurs, in part, because he is more loyal to the psychopathic Red than to anyone else he knows. It is, however, his treatment of Adeline Kelsey, a mulatto woman of forty, that truly dooms him.

Adeline Kelsey is one of the novel's most memorable minor characters. Forced into prostitution as a teenager, she escaped by attacking her pimp with "an ivory-handled springblade" (151). Subsequently, she has become a respected and influential businesswoman. A strong and independent woman, she has mastered the ability to fight against men and win. Now involved in bail bonding, she enters the novel when Ruby is in prison. Initially motivated by the blatant legal irregularities in Ruby's conviction and later by his sexual attractiveness, she gains his release just before Christmas.

Adeline then accompanies the boxer to a New York City hotel room during the holiday season. Ruby's self-destructive arrogance immediately surfaces. When he has sex with Adeline, he forces her to assume a position she considers degrading and afterward tells her that since their lovemaking meant nothing, he is returning to his wife. Enraged, Adeline rushes at Ruby with the ivory-handled springblade; but he easily disarms her and leaves the hotel room. Outside, a teenage girl calls to him, " 'Jesus loves you.' " " 'He decided to do that too late,' " Calhoun answers and hurries on (246–47).

For Ruby Calhoun, sex, like everything else in life, is a battle for dominance. Adeline Kelsey's strength, which temporarily saves him from prison and which sexually arouses him, necessitates that he humiliate her. He must never appear weak, especially to himself. A part of Ruby hates Adeline because she is a woman and because she had the power to free him. She also has the power to convict him again. Immediately after the New York hotel room scene, she begins working to achieve a second conviction for Calhoun. Largely through intimidating Nick Iello, she is successful.

At his second trial, Ruby helps Adeline Kelsey and the prosecution by stubbornly refusing to take the stand in his own defense. When Barney Kerrigan demands to know why, the boxer replies: " 'If I had to do it all over again . . . I'd do it the same way' " (304). To the reader, if not to Kerrigan, "it all" clearly refers to the hotel room incident as well as to the second trial. "It all," in fact, refers to Calhoun's life, beginning with the atrocious assault on the white homosexual. The horror that destroys Ruby Calhoun is internal as well as external. His Christmas response to the teenager's message of love arises out of the damned feeling. Ruby, in fact, is not so much committed to life as he is to a proud demand for freedom from societal repression.

Yet, one must emphasize that the reverse side of the boxer's self-destructive arrogance is an admirable pride. After the collapse of the Athens uprising, he informs Kerrigan that the prison officials still fear him: " 'I remain a threat because I remain uncrushed. I never acknowledge guilt. I dress in my own clothes here according to my own taste. I do no work. That would be an act of repentence and I have nothing to repent' " (213). In the specific context of the prison uprising, and probably the Melody Bar and Grill murders for which he was convicted, Calhoun truly has nothing to repent. He is isolated by his pride, and his pride enables him to accept that isolation.

There is, in contrast, nothing redeeming about Red Haloways. An example of man at his crummiest, Red could have been created by Céline. The light-skinned son of a proud black father, he lacks a sustaining identity. Uncertain about his racial and his sexual identities, Red Haloways is a creature of ambivalence. The novel's title comes from Dovie-Jean's assessment of Red: " 'You're like the devil's stocking. . . . You're knitted backwards' " (25). He does, in fact, bring destruction not only to himself, but to virtually everyone with whom he comes in contact.

His lack of identity is symbolized by a fondness for mimicking records by popular white singers: " 'I just don't mime *no* goddamned nigger' " (24). He wins Dovie-Jean's loyalty because he so obviously needs her—she has never felt needed before. Yet, Red's sexual insecurity necessitates his allow-ing Ruby Calhoun to take her virginity and then resenting his friend for doing so. Most importantly, it is Red's self-hatred which sets the novel's tragic events in motion.

Early in the novel, he attempts to pass for white and gets a job in Vince LeForti's Paradise bar lip-synching Frank Sinatra and Tony Bennett recordings. After the Paradise is sold to his father, Red becomes its bartender and regularly taunts LeForti whenever the former owner comes in. He specifically accuses LeForti of coming to the Paradise in search of black women. LeForti, of course, cannot understand that Red's hatred of black people equals his own. One of the first results of Red's taunting is LeForti's murder of Matt Haloways.

The novel strongly implies that Red then committed the Melody Bar and Grill murders in an insane attempt to avenge the murder of his father. Immediately after the killings, he leaves New Jersey to hide in New York City. He convinces Dovie-Jean to accompany him by overcoming her loyalty to Ruby. This is not Red's first betrayal of his boyhood friend. Algren, in fact, uses a form of allegory in the characterizations of Ruby and Red. Ruby personifies racial pride and sexual arrogance; Red embodies black self-hatred and sexual impotence. Moreover, Red is incapable of loyalty, either to principles or people. The light-skinned mimic is the boxer's Satanic alter-ego—he is, indeed, "knitted backwards."

In New York City, Red becomes a bartender at the Carousel Club and installs Dovie-Jean as a prostitute in the Playmates of Paris brothel. He expects some resentment from Dovie-Jean: " '. . . you must hate me for making a whore out of you.' " Dovie-Jean, however, has a certain sense of herself: " 'You're not making a whore out of me. I'm making a pimp out of you' " (70). For the rest of the novel, the narrative center alternates between Calhoun's trials and imprisonment and Red and Dovie-Jean's adventures in New York.

Red's inherent destructiveness is not ameliorated by New York City. In fact, he soon becomes involved in an accidental killing. When a foolish old man creates a disturbance in the Carousel, Red reaches over the bar and clips him on the side of the head. The old man crumbles lifelessly to the floor. This unpremeditated murder is, of course, reminiscent of Lefty Bicek's killing of the Greek and Frankie Machine's unplanned assault on Nifty Louie. An emptiness at the center of the Self drives each character to a desperate and fatal action.

Red's desperation is intensified when Dovie-Jean, now fully comprehending her protector's capacity for destruction, leaves him. At first, Red tries to deny his need for Dovie-Jean: "How could he need a *black* woman?" This question forces him to confront, at least momentarily, his lack of identity: "Because she was black, his heart whispered: You need her because she makes you feel *you* are black" (271). Red then enlists the aid of one Emil Moon Moonigan and begins a search for the woman who, to him, personifies self-acceptance.

Moonigan is, like Red, a repulsive creature. His personality and behavior are determined by his enormous size. Inwardly a coward, he still intimidates others. Moonigan also personifies the hypocritical puritanism Algren satirizes in *Who Lost an American?* While advocating inordinately cruel punishment of prostitutes, he admits that he patronizes them: " 'Why should I act like an animal toward my wife when I don't want her to act like an animal toward me? . . . Husband and wife aren't suppose to be animals. It's why I go with a whore once a week. Then I can return to my wife and treat her with respect and no unclean thoughts' " (190). Social class is all that prevents Moonigan from being one of Algren's third-person key-holders. He views sex as filthy and degenerate, essentially because he hates women. Patronizing society's fallen women constitutes a method of punishing himself for his own sexual drives.

When Red and Moonigan find Dovie-Jean, another unpremeditated murder occurs. Dovie-Jean taunts Moonigan about his perverse sexuality, and the desperate coward lashes out and kills her. Immediately after striking the fatal blow, "Moon looked down. He had not meant to hit that hard" (296). Now, Red must admit that he truly is the devil's stocking—he has indirectly caused the death of the only person who offered him even the illusion of an authentic Self. His insight leads only to an immediate mental and emotional collapse.

Red is last seen as a childlike creature, kept in a mental institution where he mimics popular songs on the radio and tears newspaper pages into "long, neat strips." In a powerful surrealistic scene, he is approached by "a little aging man, in his late sixties":

"I don't have to be here," the old man informed him, "I committed myself. . . . Because of the niggers. I committed myself to get away from the niggers."
"How about you?" the old man asked.
"I wanted to get away from niggers too," [Red answers].
"You always did."
"*I* always did." (306–07)

Algren does not even have to identify the old man as Vince LeForti. One sees the results of all-consuming hatred. LeForti, who killed out of racial hatred, and Red, whose self-hatred probably caused seven deaths, are joined at last in a world of shadows. Red has escaped his blackness by surrendering his manhood and his sanity.

In contrast, Dovie-Jean Dawkins has been a classic naturalistic victim; her destruction is caused by unrelenting external forces. Her mother dies when Dovie-Jean is seven or eight years old, and the girl is then forced to leave her home in the South to move in with an already-overburdened aunt in Newark. As is so often true of naturalistic victims (for example, Crane's Maggie), Dovie-Jean is victimized by her own best qualities. She has an inordinate capacity for love, but, "Nobody needed it. Nobody wanted it. Love was a drag on the market" (39). Her need for love is one aspect of her desire for life, which is undercut by her existence in a dehumanized, third-person society. Her need to love, in fact, inspires Dovie-Jean's loyalty to Red Haloways, who is virtually a parody of a man. Algren's allegory continues in the Dovie-Jean characterization—she embodies a potential for the racial pride and sexual health Red so desperately lacks. Even society's relentless assaults truly never weaken Dovie-Jean's central identity as a black woman.

She cannot escape her entrapment in a racist nation; and in one of the novel's first New York City scenes, Algren emphasizes her vulnerability, the result of an innocent faith. Taking the Circle Line boat tour around Manhattan with Red and approaching the Statue of Liberty, Dovie-Jean is profoundly moved: "The reason was simple, albeit mistaken. The girl thought she had been included among the homeless and tempest-tossed yearning to be free. She hadn't even been invited" (67). The irony of this passage reaches beyond "the girl" to include virtually all black Americans: their slave ancestors were not "invited" to America and freedom.

The extended segment of the novel concerning Dovie-Jean's experiences in the Playmates of Paris brothel recalls *Never Come Morning*'s account of Steffi R.'s existence at Mama Tomcek's and, beyond that, Kuprin's depiction of "The Pit." Algren again satirizes the hypocrisy of a society which condemns prostitutes while covertly retaining prostitution. A new thematic concern does emerge, however. *The Devil's Stocking* emphasizes more directly than any previous Algren work the johns seeking perverse gratification, the "weirdos"; and these passages often recall the last section of *Who Lost an American?:* "They are weirdos because the attraction of sex does not derive, in them, from love, but from a deep sickness of the soul. They buy secondhand copies of Playboy [*sic*] and read them secretly" (179).

Through a pseudosensational television talk show, the Uriah Yipkind Show, Algren also satirizes America's evolution into a third-person society. Any reader of Dickens, of course, catches the ironic significance of Yipkind's first name. The women of the Playmates of Paris listen in bewilderment to Yipkind's exposés of vice. They know that neither Yipkind nor his audience is truly shocked by anything that is mentioned. Algren, in fact, uses the talk-show phenomenon in general to ridicule the hypocrisy of contemporary Americans. We want, he implies, vicarious experience only. Moreover, we love to be titillated by revelations of what we already know. Talk-show regulars, especially Truman Capote, are specific targets of Algren's satire.

In this third-person world, Dovie-Jean, who needs to love, is doomed. Her alliance with Red merely sets in motion the inevitable. She cannot avoid her fatal alliance with the most dangerous "weirdo" of all. Like most of Algren's women Dovie-Jean will present a problem for feminist critics. She is, in many ways, the strongest character in the novel, but her intense need to love victimizes her. Again, Algren tended to depict women as societal victims or romantic ideals or as a combination of both.

The documentary nature of *The Devil's Stocking* generally overrides Algren's gift for ironic lyricism. Especially in the murder scenes, the novel's style is, in fact, reminiscent of Hemingway's controlled, understated narration:

> He [LeForti] pulled back the gun and fired. Haloways spun around, hit in the right shoulder. Dovie-Jean stopped dancing but the juke kept roaring. The little man pulled the gun back and fired again. The shot took off half of Matt Haloways' head.
>
> He fell across the front of the bar with his head on the bar rail. Dovie-Jean came up and stood beside Calhoun, both looking down at the old man. Neither understood.
>
> The little man understood perfectly. (51)

and:

> A bullet had caught Dude Leonard in the lower back, as if he had turned to run. He had died before he'd hit the floor.
>
> Vincio's [Vincio is another victim of the Melody Bar and Grill shootings] foot remained upon his stool's footrest. The lighted cigarette remained between his fingers. But he wasn't going to light another. (54)

Algren's unique lyricism surfaces only on the novel's last page:

> The sound of a revolver's blast was faded across the years. The people who heard it are dead, jailed or gone mad. The old faces fade; new faces take their place.

All, all is changed.
And everything remains the same. (308)

While markedly different in style from Algren's earlier novels, *The Devil's Stocking* focuses again on victims of social injustice confronting Sartrian anguish. The horror hasn't changed. Algren is, moreover, still determined to shock his readers into recognizing the essential humanity of even "the Republic's crummiest lushes." Whether or not he "went all out" in writing *The Devil's Stocking,* he created in Ruby Calhoun and Red Haloways two of his most complex and memorable characters.

Algren's fictional commitment to the urban outcast places his work in a distinct literary tradition. The Russian playwright, novelist, and short-story writer, Maxim Gorky, focused his best work on outcast city dwellers and, partially through his association with Lenin, was elevated to the unofficial position of "The Pope of Russian Literature." In conjunction with the earlier discussion of Kuprin and Céline, a brief examination of Gorky will place Algren more certainly in a tradition of literature focusing on the rejected and despised inhabitants of the city. Algren's devotion to such urban grotesques, in conjunction with his responsiveness to literary modernism, Sartrian existentialism, and the absurd, enabled him to create a unique kind of naturalism. As a result, he paved the way for such latter-day or contemporary naturalists as Hubert Selby, Jr., and John Rechy.

8

Confronting
the Horror:
Gorky, Selby,
and Rechy

*N*elson Algren included Maxim Gorky's *The Lower Depths* in a list of
works that had "lasted" for him (Corrington 132). This is not surprising
considering that the title of the play is commonly used to describe the mi-
lieu of the twentieth-century outcast. Perhaps no modern writer is as widely
associated with the lumpenproletariat as Gorky (1868–1936). His life
spanned the dramatic political upheavals which gave birth to the Soviet
Union, and his friendship with Lenin helped him become something of an
official great writer in postrevolutionary Russia. Gorky's short stories and
sketches depict the hoboes and wanderers encountered on the road in
Russia.

When produced by the Moscow Art Theater in 1902, Gorky's most successful play, *The Lower Depths,* was called *At the Bottom* and has been
translated into English under several different titles. Set entirely in a room-
ing house in an unnamed town on the Volga, the play depicts a class of
characters with which Algren must have instantly felt familiar. In an intro-
ductory note to his 1945 translation of *The Lower Depths,* Alexander
Bakshy describes the most memorable residents of Kostylyov's lodging
house as "*bsyák,* the name, literally meaning 'a barefoot,' . . . the whole
class of people who did occasional odd jobs but lived mostly by their wits.
They formed a motley, shiftless, and often criminal fringe of the population
of most Russian towns and used to be particularly numerous in port

towns." As Bakshy points out, three, if not four, of the play's main characters (the Baron, Satin, Peppel, and perhaps Luka) have spent time in jail.
These characters have developed something of a cooperative understanding with Klestch, the Tartar, and the Goiter who "typify the conscientious,
upright working man" (xxi). The stage directions for act 1 set the ironic
mood and tone of the entire play:

> A cavelike basement. A heavy vaulted ceiling, blackened with smoke, with
> patches where the plaster has fallen off. . . . Anna, lying on the bed behind the
> curtain, is heard coughing. . . . On top of the stove, unseen by the audience, the
> Actor is puttering around and coughing.
>
> It is morning in early spring. (5)

Most of the first act is devoted to the petty bickerings and quarrels of the
boarding house inhabitants, especially the male characters' taunting of the
prostitute Nastya. In this first act, Gorky establishes the cynical Satin as the
one resident of the boarding house with the potential to transcend his sur-
roundings and adopt something of an idealistic vision. Early in the play,
Satin says: "I'm tired . . . of all human words, our words. . . . I love
rare words I can't understand. When I was a boy I had a job in a telegraph
office—used to read lots of books. . . . There are some fine books—with
lots of odd words. I was an educated man, you know" (9). Satin is expressing a yearning for a new and humane vision in which to believe; and, when
the play's one stranger to Kostylyov's boarding house appears, he is
presented with precisely that. Old Luka, the sixty-year-old "pilgrim," dominates the last part of act 1 and the entire second act with his pronouncements of the need for men to have faith in, and be forgiving of, men:
". . . how can anybody cast off a human being? Whatever condition he's
in, a human being is always worth something" (24). It would be hard to find
a more concise statement of the "harsh compassion" in Algren's fiction
than this pronouncement by Luka.

Luka also lectures repeatedly that people should be concerned with the
living and not with the dead—for example, Christ. Despite the humanistic
content of his lectures, the elderly pilgrim is an ambiguous figure in the
play. The most that his message produces is some guilt and brief repentance
on the part of the boarding house residents. When the Actor is inspired by
Luka to believe that he can conquer his alcoholism, he is derided by the
other characters. The last two acts of the play moreover erase any hope for
redemption of any of Kostylyov's renters. Act 3 culminates with Peppel, a
character whose cynicism equals Satin's, lashing out at the landlord and

inadvertently killing him. Partially to taunt the other man, Peppel has not tried to hide the fact that he sleeps with Kostylyov's wife. In act 2, he says to his mistress, "I'm bored—fed up with all this business." When she asks, "Fed up with me, too?," he answers "Yes, with you too" (34). Algren must have been struck by Peppel's inadvertent murder of Kostylyov. In a comparable way, Frankie Machine is prompted by an overwhelming sense of helplessness and boredom to lash out at the drug dealer.

Critics have often said that Gorky should have followed Chekhov's advice and dropped act 4 of his play; to a degree, it is anticlimactic. Luka has departed as abruptly as he appeared, and Peppel has had to flee after the death of the landlord. Gorky utilizes the last act primarily to underscore the play's irony. While imitating Luka's "voice and manner," Satin delivers a long speech which summarizes the pilgrim's pronouncements of hope and faith:

> Lies are the religion of slaves and bosses. Truth is the god of the free man. . . . "Everybody . . . lives for something better to come. That's why we have to be considerate of every man—who knows what's in him, why he was born and what he can do? Maybe he was born for our good fortune—for our greater benefit. And most especially we have to be considerate of youngsters. . . . Don't interfere with their life. Be kind to them." (64–65)

Yet the play ends with a drunken song by Goiter, Tartar, and Bubnov ("The sun comes up, the sun goes down again—But in my cell it's never light—") and the discovery of Actor's suicide, which elicits a brutally detached response from Satin: "Ah, spoiled the song—the fool!" (73).

Any reader of Gorky's autobiographical works such as *Childhood, My Apprenticeship,* and *My Universities* can identify the source of the pervasive irony of *The Lower Depths.* More than a little revisionist thinking was, in fact, necessary before Gorky could be proclaimed the great postrevolutionary Russian writer. Throughout the three autobiographical volumes, Gorky expresses a profound ambivalence about the Russian urban lumpenproletariat as well as the peasantry. Born Alexei Peshkov, Gorky (pseudonym meaning "bitter") grew up in an oppressed and often brutal environment which determined that he could only identify with the lower classes. Still, he was constantly repelled by the senseless cruelty and meanness of spirit exhibited by those at the bottom of Russian society. Thus, throughout his autobiographical writings, Gorky expressed doubt that social reform could save those in the lower depths. Gorky's play clearly lasted for Algren. The Russian writer's vision of a lumpenproletariat tempted by but ultimately unable to accept a new humanist philosophy was echoed by

Algren in all his major fiction. More specifically, Peppel's senseless lashing out at Kostylyov undoubtedly contributed to the crucial murder scenes in *Never Come Morning* and *The Man With the Golden Arm.*

Algren, then, wrote out of a complex set of influences. Gorky as the Russian forerunner of a literature of the lumpenproletariat provided an impetus for his art; and Kuprin's account of the horror of prostitution in czarist Russia inspired the creation of an extra dimension in his fiction. In the 1940s Sartre's concepts of individual anguish and literary commitment inspired Algren to depict an internal, as well as an external, landscape of the horror. Finally, Céline's vision of the absurd helped Algren to articulate his own harsh compassion. These diverse influences enabled Algren to create a fiction based on narrative identification with rather than exploration of outwardly grotesque characters.

This narrative strategy enabled Algren to create a new naturalism—a fiction at once more brutal and more forgiving than Frank Norris's turn-of-the-century pioneering work in the genre. Donald Pizer first pointed out the philosophical vacuum at the heart of Norris's theoretical writings about naturalism. Norris, in fact, never stressed environmental determinism or any other "scientific" concept as being central to naturalism. The author of *McTeague* generally described naturalism as a form of romanticism focusing on subject matter outside the "*ordinary.*" In "Zola as a Romantic Writer," Norris insists that "the naturalist takes no note of common people," but seeks out instead the "extraordinary," the "imaginative," the "grotesque," the "monstrous," and "the tragic" (Pizer, *Literary Criticism* 71–72). Pizer accurately describes Norris's naturalism as "a fictional mode which illustrated some fundamental truth of life within a detailed presentation of the sensational and low" (*Literary Criticism* 69).

In his literary criticism, Norris also stressed the identity of the writer as moral authority. To a degree, this moral imperative of art translated for him into the championing of middle-class mores and virtues including, as Pizer has shown, "Anglo-Saxon racism." Like Jack London, Norris found in Rudyard Kipling inspiration for a vision of Anglo-Saxon economic imperialism (Pizer, *Literary Criticism* 99–100). The crowded inner cities of America with their new immigrant populations fascinated him as internal colonies of the triumphant Anglo-Saxon economic world march. Thus, in *McTeague,* he explored "the brute within" the new urban man and woman. McTeague is, in fact, Anglo-Saxon; but he is also an anachronism—a frontiersman out of place in and doomed by an increasingly foreign San Francisco. Much like the Viking heroine of *Moran of the Lady Letty,* he is too primitive to survive in a degenerate civilization.

In *McTeague,* Norris initially explores Polk Street, an accommodation street on the border between respectability and the slums, and then takes the middle-class reader on an excursion into the urban lower depths. In the course of this descent, the reader meets several grotesque personifications of the Other—Zerkow, the sadistic "redheaded Polish Jew" junkman; Maria Macapa, the half-mad woman of vaguely Spanish blood; and Trina Sieppe, whose extreme avarice inherited from her German-Swiss immigrant parents ultimately weds with her sexual masochism. Norris is presenting to the middle-class readers a gallery of grotesques, distorted nightmare projections of their own internal drives and fears. Consequently, there could be, in Norris's world, none of the complexity of characterization and symbolism, the ambiguity of motivation, which we now associate with modernist fiction. *McTeague* exemplifies the naturalistic urban novel of exploration.

With *The Man With the Golden Arm,* Nelson Algren inspired a naturalism of identification rather than exploration. Algren's Chicago is as violent and certainly as sordid as Norris's San Francisco, yet his characters are not merely exotics created as projections of the Other for a middle-class readership. In fact, by identifying with his often grotesque characters, his narrative strategy challenges the human compassion of his middle-class readers. Like Norris, Algren believed that the writer should function as a conscience of society; but the morality underlying *The Man With the Golden Arm* and *A Walk on the Wild Side* condemns the corrupt economic system which oppresses the lumpenproletariat. Algren's modernist, existentialist orientation necessitated a complexity of symbolism and character motivation which pointed to new directions for American literary naturalism. Hubert Selby, Jr., and John Rechy, among others, have followed Algren's lead in creating a complex naturalism of identification.

With the 1964 publication of *Last Exit to Brooklyn,* Hubert Selby, Jr., became a cult figure in American literature. The publication of his three subsequent novels has resulted in wider recognition; for instance, his fiction was the subject of a special 1981 issue of the *Review of Contemporary Fiction.* In *Vulnerable People,* a perceptive study of post–World War II American fiction, Josephine Hendin analyzes Selby's uniqueness: "If he does not gloat over the cruelty he describes, Selby nevertheless sees nothing else, nothing but the terror of those dismal, festering characters who spring so fully formed in their vileness from his imagination. He does write of them with love, with an energy and purity of style that is absolute in its insistence on your glimmer of recognition" (61). As June Howard points out, narrative voice in *Last Exit to Brooklyn* merges with the characters. This merger represents a new stage in the creation of a naturalism of identification. Selby documents the external landscape and internal rage of his characters with a cold, terrifying detachment. As Hendin says, Selby focuses so exclusively on violence and cruelty that his world becomes a surrealistic nightmare. Unlike Algren, he does not soften the horror with comedy or lyricism. Still, the underlying assumption of his fiction is comparable to that of *The Man With the Golden Arm* and especially *A Walk on the Wild Side*. Selby's unrelenting narrative focus demands a recognition of his characters' essential humanity, despite the brutality of their actions. His four novels further the wedding of naturalistic technique with a Céline-inspired vision of the absurd. The people who inhabit Selby's world are, in fact, more immediately terrifying than such Algren creations as Nubby O'Neill, Nifty Louie, Blind Pig, Oliver Finnerty, and Red Haloways.

Initially, the world of *Last Exit to Brooklyn* seems a recreation of the most familiar landscape of American literary realism. Selby, like Norris, Crane, and Algren, is concerned with the mean streets of urban life. *Last Exit* is divided into four parts and a coda; a Brooklyn street gang unifies the book's episodic structure. The unrelenting brutality of Selby's gang members places them in a surreal universe that even Algren's "crummiest lushes" would hardly recognize. Every episode in the novel is dominated by horror, but Selby's coldly detached documentation of brutality makes four of them especially unforgettable.

"The Queen is Dead" describes the sadistic humiliation of a drag queen, Georgette, by members of the street gang. When the episode ends, Georgette is not in fact dead; but the degradation she has experienced is arguably worse than death. The nightmare vision, central to American letters since Brockden Brown and Poe, has never been more frighteningly presented than in "Tralala." In this brief segment, Tralala, a cold, calculating prostitute, is gang-raped and murdered. Selby's technique can be clearly distinguished from Algren's by contrasting the gang rape of Tralala to the comparable ordeal of Steffi R. in *Never Come Morning*. While Algren keeps his narrative focus on Lefty's reactions to Steffi's pain, Selby documents the ever-accelerating horror of Tralala's destruction: ". . . Tralala lying naked covered with blood urine and semen and a small blot forming on the seat between her legs as blood seeped from her crotch" (116). As Hendin points out, Selby's characters hate women and long to take out their rage, either in reality or fantasy, on a female, any female. They hate women because, like Algren's third-person key-holders, they hate life, and they hate themselves.

The longest section in *Last Exit,* "Strike," describes the horror experienced by Harry, a union strike organizer, when he at last confronts his latent homosexuality. Unable to stop himself, he begins seeking out homosexual contacts, while proclaiming his hatred of "queers." Finally, he turns to members of the street gang, who brutally torture him. Homosexuality, and any male expression of androgyny, is instantly punished in Selby's world.

Overt acts of violence are largely absent from "Landsend," *Last Exit*'s coda. Verbal and environmental dehumanization take their place. In unrelenting detail, Selby documents the filth and despair of life in a Brooklyn housing project. Here, the horror derives primarily from the clear implication that such an environment is a constant, beyond possibility of change. Once again, the true horror is day-to-day existence—"the horror is that there is no horror." Throughout *Last Exit to Brooklyn*, environmental determinism is such a given that there is no boundary between setting and character.

In contrast, there is no clear external reality in Selby's second novel, *The Room* (1971), and the traditional naturalistic role of environment is thus irrelevant. Reminiscent in form of Genet's *Our Lady of the Flowers*, *The Room* recounts the sadistic fantasies of a man imprisoned for an unspecified crime. The novel is an uninterrupted expression of insane hatred and lust for revenge. The police officers who arrested the central character are the initial targets of his brutal fantasies. Soon, however, his fantasy exceeds them and includes an imagined female victim of police brutality. The madman hallucinates, in horrific detail, virtually every conceivable form of physical torture and degradation—rape, beatings, forced fellatio and sodomy, bestiality, and mutilation. He either imagines himself torturing and dehumanizing the police officers or their vicious assault of the imaginary woman. There is probably no more excruciating portrait of the psychopathic mind in American literature than *The Room*.

In the last analysis, the madman's hatred is self-directed, arising out of a sense of powerlessness. Selby's idea is hardly new—like so many characters in contemporary fiction, his creation is intimidated by his helplessness in the face of the anonymous authority of bureaucracies. What is new is Selby's prolonged exploration of the displaced rage that results from such intimidation. His sense of powerlessness necessitates that the prisoner invent a woman as victim. Like most of Selby's males, he can only associate weakness with the female. He must transfer his own vulnerability to a woman, even if it is necessary to invent one.

For different reasons than in *The Room*, environmental determinism is not a significant factor in *The Demon* (1976). In this novel, for the first time, Selby focuses on the upper middle class. The external reality in *The Demon* is that of modern office buildings, executives' picnics, and suburban mansions. The main character, Harry White, is a young, upwardly mobile junior executive. White is better than good at what he does—he is, in fact, a genius at designing original and far-reaching innovations for his company. All that stands in the way of his swift ascension to the top of the corporate ladder is "the demon."

Initially, the demon manifests itself in Harry's emotionless seductions of women—women he does not know but hopes are married. For Harry, a central ingredient of the excitement of his sexual games is the danger of being caught by an irate and possibly violent husband. While no vengeful husband appears, this uncontrollable behavior takes its toll in an unexpected way. Harry is unable to concentrate on his work and loses a promotion to a clearly inferior co-worker. In desperation, he then marries, hoping to subdue the demon through this social convention.

Soon after his marriage, however, Harry's demon reappears, this time in sexual and nonsexual transgressions. Unfaithful to his wife, he is drawn to overtly criminal behavior, moving rapidly from petty shoplifting to major theft. It is still the element of danger, of being caught and disgraced, that most excites him. Again, he escapes any suspicion of wrongdoing, and the demon's demands accelerate. Finally, in a scene of unforgettable horror, Harry murders, pushing an anonymous man in front of a speeding subway train.

Harry's demon clearly originates in an apparently sourceless and pervasive guilt. It is a guilt much like Frankie Machine's—not the result of any single incident, it originates in a profound awareness of the nothingness which lies at the heart of the Self. The unknown man embodies Harry White's own lack of identity, yet even murder will not appease this insistent internal horror.

The ending of *The Demon* is forced and obvious; it is the one time when Selby dramatizes his existential vision in allegorical terms. After a second anonymous murder, Harry decides that he must kill Cardinal Leterman, a beloved spokesman for the church who has survived a heart attack only after being momentarily pronounced dead. He fatally stabs the clergyman during a Resurrection Mass in St. Patrick's Cathedral and miraculously escapes only to drown himself. Selby is in part dramatizing Nietzsche's "murder" of God; Harry White kills the resurrected savior. The dedication of the novel reveals, however, some additional complexity: "This book is dedicated / to / Bill, / who has helped me learn / I must surrender to win." In *The Demon,* Selby moves closer to a variation of Christian existentialism. Harry's drowning is a surrender, a baptism which represents the only escape from the demon, the void at the core of being.

A brilliant experiment in collective narration, *Requiem for a Dream* (1979) is a harrowing tale of addiction and its consequences. The novel's pace is rapid, at times breathtaking, and its language reflects the idioms of its characters. Three young New Yorkers, Harry, Tyrone, and Marion, dream of obtaining a pound of pure heroin; nearby, Harry's mother, Sara, lives only through the shadowy figures on her television screen. The novel's beginning foreshadows the fates of all four characters—Harry steals and sells his mother's television to get money for drugs and then, along with Tyrone, Marion, and others, gets high in a morgue.

These opening scenes are followed by an extended sequence during which it appears that all four characters might realize their dream. Harry, a Jewish-American, and Tyrone, a young black man, successfully break into the New York City drug traffic. Marion, the daughter of upper-class white Christian parents, then moves in with Harry. Her TV set recovered, Sara resumes her vicarious existence until she receives a letter informing her that she might be a future contestant on a television quiz show. For Sara, this hypothetical future becomes an intensely real present, and she begins living only for the promised fame.

In fact, the inevitable destruction of all four characters has been set in motion. At first occasionally, then regularly, Harry, Tyrone, and Marion begin using, instead of selling, their heroin. Their addictions intensify as the New York drug supply dries up. During the panic, each betrays the other two by withholding small amounts of heroin from the common supply. Ultimately, Marion is reduced to prostitution, and Harry and Tyrone begin a desperate journey to Miami in search of their pound of pure. Southern racists arrest the two New Yorkers for vagrancy before they reach the Florida border. Each suffers a nightmarish fate: at the time of the arrest, Harry is in unbearable pain from gangrene in his arm, resulting from careless use of the needle, and is last seen awaiting amputation of the diseased limb, while Tyrone is sentenced to a chain gang where his identity as a black New York drug addict provokes unrelenting torture.

From the moment she receives her letter, Sara begins taking diet pills in a desperate attempt to look "Zophtic," "like Rita Hayworth." Soon addicted to the pills, she refuses to acknowledge that the television people have forgotten her. Gradual, self-imposed starvation and desperation over her mysteriously disappearing dream reduce her to an infantile state, perpetuated by the uncaring bureaucracy of a charity hospital.

In *Requiem for a Dream,* Selby spares no detail in documenting the horrors experienced by his four characters. Again, the novel is headed by biblical quotations, the most significant being Psalm 127:1: "Except the Lord build the house, they labor in vain that build it. . . ." Harry, Tyrone, Marion, and Sara demonstrate the impossibility of finding any substitute for salvation in a godless world. Addiction supplants faith; heroin becomes "the Host"; and television quiz shows replace communion. Impersonal institutions complete the modern nightmare.

The first memorable treatment of drug addiction in American fiction was *The Man With the Golden Arm*. Beyond Algren's having introduced this subject matter into serious American literature, Selby owes his predecessor a greater debt. He too wishes to shock his readers into a recognition of the essential humanity of socially despised and often brutal characters— the street gang of *Last Exit to Brooklyn*, the insane prisoner in *The Room*, the businessman who kills God in *The Demon*, and *Requiem for a Dream*'s victims of addiction. In fact, Selby's surrealistic naturalism was first anticipated in American fiction by *A Walk on the Wild Side*. Selby may have learned from it, as well as from Céline, how to depict a horror that seems too hideous to be real, but which undeniably exists.

Not uncommonly linked with Selby by reviewers and critics, John Rechy achieved considerable recognition for his first novel, *City of Night* (1963). Rechy's work also documents the futile search for redemption in a world without God—he has said, in fact, that the phrase, "no substitute for salvation" will appear in each of his books (Giles 21). Like that of Algren and Selby, his work evokes recognition of the humanness of a despised group. With two exceptions (*The Vampire* in 1971 and *The Fourth Angel* in 1973), his seven novels focus on America's homosexual underground, whose inhabitants Rechy has described as an alienated nobility: ". . . there's no more alienated figure than the homosexual. It's the only minority against whose existence there are laws. There's no law against being black, or Jewish, or anything else; but there are laws against being homosexual. . . . The homosexual is the clearest symbol of alienation and despair. And nobility" (Giles 21).

City of Night is based on a quest—a "youngman" leaves El Paso, Texas and begins a search for salvation which takes him to New York City, Los Angeles, Chicago, San Francisco, and New Orleans. No salvation is to be found in a nighttime world of hustlers, gay bars, and drag queens. Rechy focuses primarily on the hustler's experience, an endless pursuit of "numbers" of emotionless homosexual contacts. Inspired by Dos Passos and Steinbeck, the novel's structure is that of a series of isolated stories connected by "chapters" focusing on the central character. This structure conveys the urban isolation of the homosexual.

A childhood memory of the relentless west Texas wind uncovering the decaying body of his dead dog haunts the youngman narrator. He cannot escape the living nightmare of his early glimpse of the final absurdity of death and decay, of time and materiality. In an interview, Rechy has commented on the symbolic significance of the narrator's memory of seeing the decaying body of his dog: ". . . this is the narrator's first contact with the existential horror . . . when you exclude the soul—when you see the body rotting after death—all there is is death; not only death, but . . . physical decay. . . . Symbolically, the boy's innocence is buried when the dog is re-buried, decaying, soulless" (Giles 26–27). Collecting numbers of anonymous sexual contacts momentarily affirms his virility, and thus his being, but it can offer only an illusionary escape from the inevitability of death. The youngman's attempt to create a viable essence of being-for-itself by repeatedly penetrating the bodies of nameless others with his penis is, of course, doomed. By attempting to make an unfeeling sexual virility the basis of a Self, the youngman has, in fact, entrapped himself in another dimension of the temporal.

The style and technique of Rechy's first novel are closer than Selby's to Algren. The connecting chapters are distinguished by a lyricism of pain and despair, which especially recall *The Man With the Golden Arm* and *A Walk on the Wild Side*. The grotesque comedy of the novel also alleviates the horror, while simultaneously intensifying it. Like Frankie Machine and Ruby Calhoun, Rechy's unforgettable characters are condemned by respectable society and their own guilt. Miss Destiny, the outrageous drag queen, longs for a fabulous Hollywood wedding; the married man from Santa Monica attempts to deny his homosexual desires; and Kathy, the incredibly beautiful drag queen, revenges herself against the masculine culture that has made her an outcast. All three, like the youngman from El Paso, are in flight from the ultimate absurdity, death and its obscene decay.

An existential vision is even more overtly emphasized in Rechy's second novel, *Numbers* (1967). In it, the main character, Johnny Rio, journeys from Laredo, Texas to Los Angeles determined to have thirty anonymous sexual encounters in ten days. In the opening sequence, Rechy quickly establishes that the concept of "numbers" has dimensions beyond those initially anticipated by Johnny Rio. Driving toward Los Angeles, he thinks of the idea of one's "number" coming up: "He imagines God poised behind an automatic rifle sniping each 'number' down—though, on occasion, He might, for expediency, use a machine gun to topple the ranks like dominoes" (13). Johnny's obsession with death is related to "a harrowing sensitivity about age" (17). For the homosexual hustler, age threatens a loss of attractiveness and thus a diminution of the essential Self. Like the youngman in *City of Night,* Johnny Rio's code makes him vulnerable to an added dimension of time.

Moreover, just as he nears his goal of sexual contacts, a friend points out to Johnny the true significance of the number which he has chosen—" '30 is a printer's term for The End' " (231). For the remainder of the novel, Johnny is relentlessly pursued by death. Sexual contacts no longer represent an uncomplicated reassurance of vitality for him—instead, they bring him closer to "The End." Ultimately, all Johnny can do is to go beyond thirty, to search repeatedly for "just one more number" (253). Such desperation is inevitably doomed to failure, and the novel ends with Johnny confronting the very personification of death.

In *Numbers,* Rechy creates out of the American frontier myth an ironic subtext for his novel. Johnny Rio sounds like the name of a Western gun fighter, and it is moreover an adopted name. While "hunting" in Los Angeles' Griffith Park, Johnny always parks so that his Texas license plates can be easily seen. Yet, Johnny leaves Texas, the heart of cowboy mythology, to go farther west. He goes to the last frontier of so much American idealism—Los Angeles and southern California. California and particularly Los Angeles as Eden corrupted are such a pervasive image in American letters (for example, in Steinbeck, Nathanael West, Raymond Chandler) that Rechy does not even have to develop this metaphoric subtext.

After *City of Night, Bodies and Souls* (1983) is Rechy's best novel (his 1988 *Marilyn's Daughter* was published too late for evaluation here). He returns to the short story structure of the earlier novel to depict another surrealistic world, again embodied in the city of Los Angeles with its maze of intersections leading everywhere except to the soul. Another gallery of the condemned emerges: Amber, a pornographic film star struggling to accept her exploitation; Hester Washington, a proud and angry black woman fighting against the racist degradation of Watts; Dave Clinton, a male stripper seeking punishment in a homosexual "slave auction"; and Sister Woman, a false voice of salvation. The connecting chapters recount the apocalyptic odyssey of three young people who embody the dark reality lurking beneath the surface of America's dominant mythologies. As in *Numbers,* Rechy largely abandons the grotesque comedy of *City of Night* in *Bodies and Souls* while retaining the despairing lyricism of his first novel.

Rechy's and Selby's fiction evokes Algren's best work. All three writers communicate a naturalist vision of urban grotesques with a modernist, existential technique stressing Sartrian anguish and a harsh, unrelenting sense of the absurd. Like Zola, all three challenge the middle-class reader's assumptions about the very nature of humanity. For the horror that Algren's, Selby's, and Rechy's fiction confronts is not ultimately so foreign as it seems. Hassan, among others, has described the alienation of everyone in the postwar world—World War II, the Holocaust, and the bomb brought the vulnerability and insignificance of the individual to the forefront of contemporary consciousness. People do not think of themselves as living in a universe of labyrinths and mirrors; and, in our media-saturated world, drug addiction, the brutality of the ghetto, and even the homosexual underground are not unfamiliar territories. Moreover, Selby and Rechy are not the only inheritors of the Algren legacy. A comparable authorial focus and narrative tone can be found in William Kennedy's Pulitzer Prize–winning *Ironweed* (1983), Joyce Carol Oates's *them* (1969), and in the award-winning films of Martin Scorsese. The lowercase title of Oates's work, for example, reflects an ironic authorial awareness of the traditional relationship between middle-class reader and "grotesque" naturalistic characters. "them," in Oates's novel, refers to the urban poor vaguely sensed as manifestations of the Other by the middle and upper-middle classes. A central tension in the novel is that between the inhabitants of inner-city Detroit and those products of the city's wealthy suburbs who chance to encounter "them."

Nelson Algren's imagination was always wide-ranging and daring. The critical neglect of his role in shaping a new kind of fiction was in part due to Algren himself. He created the persona of an uneducated midwesterner who, despite his well-known associations with Sartre and de Beauvoir, had never heard of existentialism. Moreover, his bitterness over others' neglect and distortion of his work limited his fictional output and blinded him to important ramifications of much that he did produce. It was apparently always difficult for him to believe in his vision sufficiently to "go all out" and attempt a major work. Still, what he did produce paved the way for significant innovations in contemporary fiction and film.

In recent years, the acceptable canon of twentieth-century American literature has been challenged by black and feminist critics among others. New Criticism's assumptions about the necessity or even the possibility of literature's isolation from society and history are increasingly being reexamined. Such scholarly studies as June Howard's *Form and History in American Literary Naturalism* and Walter Benn Michaels's *The Gold Standard and the Logic of Naturalism* (1987) are evidence of an interest in redefining the genre of naturalism. Hopefully, an increased awareness of what Howard calls latter-day naturalism and of Algren's role in its evolution will result from this period of critical challenge.

Several months ago, I spent an afternoon in Chicago's Water Tower Place, a dazzling structure which might have emerged from the mind of F. Scott Fitzgerald. The tower is a multilevel creation inside which one enters a glass elevator and ascends to ever more expensive stores and specialty shops. Everything one might want and a great deal that only a few people could have imagined are inside Water Tower Place. The glass elevator ride is a tantalizing journey toward a material heaven; in a real sense, it is Fitzgerald's moment "commensurate with man's capacity for wonder."

On the way to the Water Tower, I passed, on a side street, a crippled black beggar who gave me a look of recognition, laughed, and said, "It gets inside your head. *You* know that. It gets inside your head." I, of course, did not know precisely what "it" referred to, but I knew what he meant. He meant the "horror."

It has since occurred to me that a metafictional writer might best capture the essence of Water Tower Place. Its display of the material transcends the usual adjectives. It is not precisely lavish, excessive, ostentatious, gaudy, or extravagant. Above all, it is extremely attractive. Increasingly, our most familiar reality is that of the shopping center, of which Water Tower Place is ultimately no more and no less than one spectacular example. Such a world was created to anticipate every need of economically secure middle- and upper-class Americans. One can eat in expensive or not-so-expensive restaurants; one can buy designer telephones, fur coats, carved animals from Kenya, and word processors inside Water Tower. One can also purchase the novels of Algren, Rechy, and Selby and see live performances of Tennessee Williams plays. Truly, there is little real necessity for leaving the shopping-center world. In a store called "Accent Chicago," one can purchase enough Windy City souvenirs that there is almost no point is seeing any more of the city. Most important, any thought of death would seem foreign, even unnatural, inside Water Tower Place.

But, if one wanders outside the shopping-center world, the side streets and the crippled beggars are still there. The lasting value of Nelson Algren grows out of his conviction that these mean streets are also reality and that these beggars are as human as all of us. His novels utilize brutal description, broad humor, and a uniquely despairing lyricism to tell us that this city is, indeed, eternal. Ultimately, the horror *will* get in our heads. No ascension on a glass elevator can negate the absurdity of our mortality. Algren's fiction does contain a moral—the only meaningful human victories are won by individuals who strive for an authentic Self in the face of this final absurdity.

Bibliography

Algren, Nelson. *The Devil's Stocking*. New York: Arbor House, 1983.

———. *The Man With the Golden Arm*. Garden City, N.Y.: Doubleday, 1949.

———. *The Neon Wilderness*. New York: Hill and Wang, 1960.

———. *Never Come Morning*. New York: Harper, 1942.

———. *Somebody in Boots*. New York: Farrar, Straus and Giroux, 1935.

———. *A Walk on the Wild Side*. New York: Farrar, Straus and Cudahy, 1956.

———. *Who Lost an American?* New York: Macmillan, 1963.

Allsop, K., ed. "A Talk on the Wild Side." *Spectator* 203 (16 Oct. 1959): 509–10.

Anderson, Alston, and Terry Southern. "Nelson Algren." *Paris Review* 11 (Winter 1955): 37–58.

Barrett, William. *Irrational Man: A Study in Existential Philosophy*. 1958. Garden City, N.Y.: Anchor, 1962.

Barth, John. "The Literature of Exhaustion." *The American Novel Since World War II*. Ed. Marcus Klein. Greenwich, Conn.: Fawcett, 1969. 267–79. Rpt. from *Atlantic Monthly* 220 (Aug. 1967): 29–34.

Bluestone, George. "Nelson Algren." *Western Review* 22 (Autumn 1957): 27–44.

Bone, Robert A. *The Negro Novel in America*. 1958. Rev. ed. New Haven: Yale University Press, 1965.

Borges, Jorge Luis. *Labyrinths: Selected Stories and Other Writings*. New York: New Directions, 1964.

Brée, Germaine. *Camus and Sartre: Crisis and Commitment*. New York: Delacorte, 1972.

Bibliography

Breit, Harvey. "The Writer Observed." *The Writer Observed*. Cleveland: World Publishing, 1956. Rpt. from *New York Times Book Review* 2 Oct. 1949: 33.

Bruccoli, Matthew J. *Nelson Algren: A Descriptive Bibliography*. Pittsburgh: University of Pittsburgh Press, 1985. (With the assistance of Judith Baughman.)

Camus, Albert. *The Myth of Sisyphus and Other Essays*. Trans. Justin O'Brien. New York: Random House, 1955.

Céline, Louis-Ferdinand. *Journey to the End of the Night*. 1934. Trans. Ralph Manheim. New York: New Directions, 1983.

Cohen-Solal, Annie. *Sartre: A Life*. New York: Pantheon Books, 1987.

Corrington, John William. "Nelson Algren Talks with NOR's Editor-at-Large." *New Orleans Review* 1 (Winter 1969): 130–32.

Cowley, Malcolm. *The Literary Situation*. 1954. New York: Viking, 1958.

Cox, Martha Heasley, and Wayne Chatterton. *Nelson Algren*. Boston: G. K. Hall, 1975.

Donohue, H. E. F. *Conversations with Nelson Algren*. New York: Hill and Wang, 1964.

Eisinger, Chester E. *Fiction of the Forties*. Chicago: University of Chicago Press, 1963.

Fiedler, Leslie. "The Noble Savages of Skid Row." *Reporter* 15 (12 July 1956): 43–44.

Frohock, W. M. *The Novel of Violence in America*. Dallas: Southern Methodist University Press, 1957.

Geismar, Maxwell. *American Moderns: From Rebellion to Conformity*. New York: Hill and Wang, 1958.

Gelfant, Blanche H. *The American City Novel*. Norman: University of Oklahoma Press, 1954.

Giles, James R., with Wanda H. Giles. "An Interview with John Rechy." *Chicago Review* 25 (1973): 19–31.

Gilman, Sander L. *Difference and Pathology: Stereotypes of Sexuality, Race, and Madness*. Ithaca, N.Y.: Cornell University Press, 1985.

Gleason, Ralph J. "Perspectives: Is It Out of Control?" *Rolling Stone* 6 Aug. 1970: 9.

Gorky, Maxim. *Childhood*. Trans. Margaret Wettlin. Moscow: Progress Publishers, 1954.

———. *The Lower Depths and Other Plays*. Trans. Alexander Bakshy. New Haven: Yale University Press, 1945.

———. *My Apprenticeship. My Universities*. Trans. Margaret Wettlin. Moscow: Progress Publishers, 1954.

Hassan, Ihab. *Radical Innocence: The Contemporary American Novel*. Princeton, N.J.: Princeton University Press, 1961.

Hendin, Josephine. *Vulnerable People: A View of American Fiction Since 1945*. Oxford: Oxford University Press, 1978.

Howard, June. *Form and History in American Literary Naturalism*. Chapel Hill: University of North Carolina Press, 1985.

Jones, James. *Some Came Running*. New York: Charles Scribner's Sons, 1957.

Bibliography

Kleppner, Paul. *Chicago Divided: The Making of a Black Mayor.* DeKalb: Northern Illinois University Press, 1985.

Kuprin, Alexandre. *Yama, or the Pit.* Trans. Bernard Guilbert Guerney. New York: Modern Library, 1932.

La Capra, Dominick. *A Preface to Sartre.* Ithaca, N.Y.: Cornell University Press, 1978.

Lehan, Richard. "American Literary Naturalism: The French Connection." *Nineteenth-Century Fiction* 38 (Spring 1984): 529–57.

Lipton, Lawrence. "A Voyeur's View of the Wild Side: Nelson Algren and His Reviewers." *Chicago Review Anthology* Winter 1957: 31–41.

Marcel, Gabriel. *The Philosophy of Existentialism.* 1956. Secaucus, N.J.: The Citadel Press, 1980. (Copyright 1956 by Philosophical Library, Inc.)

Mailer, Norman. *Advertisements for Myself.* New York: G. P. Putnam's Sons, 1959.

Michaels, Walter Benn. *The Gold Standard and the Logic of Naturalism.* Berkeley: University of California Press, 1987.

Oates, Joyce Carol. *them.* New York: Vanguard, 1969.

Pintauro, Joe. "Algren in Exile." *Chicago* 37 (Feb. 1988): 92–101, 156–63.

Pizer, Donald, ed. *The Literary Criticism of Frank Norris.* Austin: University of Texas Press, 1964.

———. "Stephen Crane's *Maggie* and American Naturalism." *Criticism* 7 (Spring 1965): 168–75.

———. *Twentieth-Century American Literary Naturalism: An Introduction.* Carbondale: Southern Illinois University Press, 1982.

Podhoretz, Norman. "The Man With the Golden Beef." *New Yorker* 32 (2 June 1956): 132, 134, 137–39.

Rahv, Philip. "Notes on the Decline of Naturalism." *The American Novel Since World War II.* Ed. Marcus Klein. Greenwich, Conn.: Fawcett, 1969. 27–38. Rpt. from Philip Rahv, *Image and Idea.* New York: New Directions, 1957.

Ray, David, ed. "Talk on the Wild Side: A Bowl of Coffee with Nelson Algren." *Reporter* 20 (11 June 1959): 31–33.

Rayner, John D. "Nelson Algren and Simone de Beauvoir: The End of Their Affair at Miller, Indiana." *The Old Northwest* 5 (1979–80): 401–07.

Rechy, John. *Bodies and Souls.* New York: Carroll & Graf, 1983.

———. *City of Night.* New York: Grove, 1963.

———. *Marilyn's Daughter.* New York: Carroll & Graf, 1988.

———. *Numbers.* New York: Grove, 1967.

Roth, Philip. "Writing American Fiction." *The American Novel Since World War II.* Ed. Marcus Klein. Greenwich, Conn.: Fawcett, 1969. 142–58. Rpt. from *Commentary* 31 (Mar. 1961): 223–33.

Sartre, Jean-Paul. *Being and Nothingness.* 1956. Trans. Hazel E. Barnes. New York: Washington Square Press, n.d.

———. *Literature and Existentialism.* 1949. Trans. Barnard Frechtman. Secaucus, N.J.: The Citadel Press, 1980. Original title: *What is Literature?*

———. *Nausea.* Trans. Lloyd Alexander. New York: New Directions, 1954.

Bibliography

Seelye, John. "The Night Watchman." *Chicago* 37 (Feb. 1988): 69–70, 72.

Selby, Hubert, Jr. *The Demon.* Chicago: Playboy Press, 1976.

_____. *Last Exit to Brooklyn.* 1964. New York: Grove, 1965.

_____. *Requiem for a Dream.* Chicago: Playboy Press, 1978.

_____. *The Room.* New York: Grove, 1971.

Studing, Richard. "Researching and Collecting Nelson Algren." *American Book Collector* 3 (Jan.–Feb. 1986): 32–37.

Tanner, Tony. *City of Words.* London: Jonathan Cape, 1971.

Walcutt, Charles Child. *American Literary Naturalism: A Divided Stream.* Minneapolis: University of Minnesota Press, 1956.

Index

Index

Index